Chemistry
Connecting Students to Science Series

By
DR. BARBARA R. SANDALL

COPYRIGHT © 2002 Mark Twain Media, Inc.

ISBN 1-58037-213-9

Printing No. CD-1559

Mark Twain Media, Inc., Publishers
Distributed by Carson-Dellosa Publishing Company, Inc.

Table of Contents

Introduction to the Series

The Connecting Students to Science Series is designed for grades 5–8+. This series will introduce the following topics: Simple Machines, Electricity and Magnetism, Rocks and Minerals, Atmosphere and Weather, Chemistry, Light and Color, Sound, and The Solar System. Each book will contain an introduction to the topic, naive concepts, inquiry activities, content integration, children's literature connections, curriculum resources, assessment documents, and a bibliography and materials list. Students will develop an understanding of the concepts and processes of science through the use of good scientific techniques. Students will be engaged in higher-level thinking skills while doing fun and interesting activities. All of the activities will be aligned with the National Science Education Standards (NSES) and National Council of Teachers of Mathematics (NCTM) Standards.

This series is written for classroom teachers, parents, families, and students. The books in this series can be used as a full unit of study or as individual lessons to supplement existing textbooks or curriculum programs. Activities are designed to be pedagogically sound, hands-on, minds-on science activities that support the NSES. Parents and students can use this series as an enhancement to what is being done in the classroom or as a tutorial at home. The procedures and content background are clearly explained in the introduction and within the individual activities. Materials used in the activities are commonly found in classrooms and homes.

If teachers are giving letter grades for the activities, points may be awarded for each level of mastery indicated on the assessment rubrics. If not, simple check marks at the appropriate levels will give students feedback on how well they are doing.

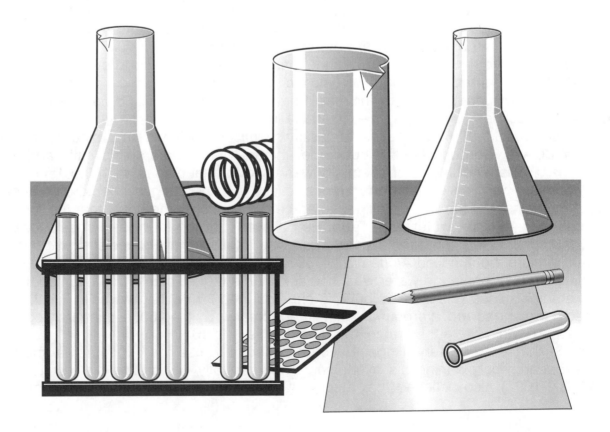

Introduction to the Concepts/Topic Area

Historical Perspective

Science as an organized body of knowledge began with the Ionian School of Greek philosophers.

Alchemy, one of the earliest forms of chemistry, combines religion, science, philosophy, and magic. It developed in Alexandria, Egypt; China, and Greece sometime after the sixth century B.C. Archimedes (287–212 B.C.) discovered the **law of buoyancy** called **Archimedes' Principle**. Archimedes' Principle states that an object placed in a liquid seems to lose an amount of weight equal to the amount of fluid it displaces. Archimedes conducted an experiment to determine how much gold was in the king's crown. He did so by measuring the amount of water the crown displaced when it was submerged in water. If the crown displaced the same amount of water as an equal volume of gold, he could determine if the crown was made of pure gold.

Democritus (460–370 B.C.) developed the **atomic theory of matter**, which states that all substances in the universe are made of particles that could not be broken down further. Later, these particles were called **atoms**, which is a Greek word meaning "indivisible." Democritus also explained that atoms could not be created or destroyed but could be rearranged in different combinations. This was the beginning of the development of the **law of conservation of mass and energy**.

Alchemy arrived in A.D. 300 and was the main source of chemical knowledge until 1600. Some of the discoveries made during this time included producing chemical changes in natural substances, improving methods for taking metal from ores, making and using acids, and designing balances and crucibles. Alchemy spread to Arabia in A.D. 642.

Arrazi (A.D. 880–909) was the first to classify chemical substances into mineral, vegetable, animal, and derivative groups. He also subdivided minerals into metals, spirits, salts, and stones.

In the 1500s, knowledge of chemistry was used to fight diseases. In the 1500–1600s, some alchemists were called **iatrochemists** because they had begun to study the chemical effects of medicines on the body. Philippus Paracelsus accepted the belief that the four basic substances were air, fire, water, and earth. He believed that the four basic substances were made of mercury, sulfur, and salt. Libavius, who was a follower of Paracelsus, wrote the first accurate chemistry book called *Alchemia* in 1597. Jan Baptista van Helmont believed only air and water were elements, and water was the basic element of all plants. He invented the word *gas* and studied gases released by burning charcoal and fermenting wine. In 1592, Galileo developed a **thermoscope**, a precursor to the thermometer. By the 1600s, chemistry became a science. Jean Beguin wrote the first textbook of chemistry in 1611.

In the thirteenth century, Roger Bacon had begun to use the experimental method of chemical research by planning his experiments and carefully interpreting his results. Robert Boyle (1627–1691) also believed that theory must be supported by experimentation. Boyle

Introduction to the Concepts/Topic Area (cont.)

continued Van Helmont's study of gases, and through his experiments found that air, earth, fire, and water were not elements. The publication of his book, *The Sceptical Chymist* (1661), was the beginning of the end of alchemy. In 1662, Boyle discovered that there is an inverse relationship between the volume of a gas and its pressure, now referred to as Boyle's Law. Boyle also rejected the current thought that matter was made of earth, air, water, and fire. He proposed that matter consisted of primary particles that could collect together to make what he called "corpuscles."

During the 1700s, many elements were discovered, including oxygen and its role in chemical reactions. This was one of the keys to modern chemistry.

Joseph Priestly (1733–1804) conducted research on gases and discovered what would later be called **oxygen**. He found that materials burned readily in oxygen, and it had an invigorating effect if it was inhaled. He also discovered what we now know as **carbon dioxide**. While living next door to a brewery, he discovered that the fermentation of grain gave off a gas that was heavier than air and put out fire. He also discovered that when it was mixed with water, it made a refreshing drink, soda water, which was the precursor to present-day soft drinks.

Antoine-Laurent Lavoisier (1743–1794) is considered the founder of modern chemistry because of his strict approach to research. He drew up the first rational system of chemical nomenclature. He also studied combustion, and when he heard of the gas that encouraged the burning process, he called it oxygen. He defined burning as the uniting of a substance with oxygen.

During the 1800s, fifty elements were discovered. Sir Humphry Davy discovered sodium and potassium by running electricity through substances containing them. This process was called **electrolysis**. He also experimented with gases and discovered nitrous oxide and its properties; however, he is most well known for inventing a safety lamp for miners.

Friedrich Wohler's (1800–1882) research developed the concepts of organic and inorganic chemistry. He and Justus von Liebig discovered that the spatial organization of atoms within a molecule was important in determining the kind of substance it made. Chemistry was later divided into three main branches: inorganic, organic, and physical chemistry. **Inorganic chemistry** is the study of compounds without carbon. **Organic chemistry** is the study of substances containing carbon. **Physical chemistry** deals with the study of heat, electricity, and other forms of energy in chemical processes.

In 1808, John Dalton published an atomic theory suggesting that each element was made up of a certain kind of atom, and each was different from all other elements. His atomic weights were not correct; however, he did formulate the Atomic Theory of Matter. The **Atomic Theory of Matter** states that all matter is made up of atoms. His theories were based on three propositions: (1) All matter is made of extremely small indivisible particles called atoms; (2) Atoms of one element are exactly alike; and (3) When elements combine, they form compounds—their atoms combine in simple numerical proportions.

In 1828, Jöns Berzelius calculated more accurate atomic weights based on Dalton's atomic theory and Joseph Louis Gay-Lussac's (1778–1850) **Law of Combining Volumes**. This law states that elements combine in definite proportions by volume to form compounds. Berzelius also introduced the use of **atomic symbols**.

Amedeo Avogadro in 1811 discovered that there was a difference between atoms and molecules. Stanislao Cannizzaro demonstrated how Avogadro's theory applied to the measurement of atomic weights. This work led to the Periodic Law developed by Dmitri Mendeleev

Introduction to the Concepts/Topic Area (cont.)

and Lothar Meyer in 1869. The **Periodic Law** states that an element's properties depend upon its atomic weight. Mendeleev developed this discovery into the periodic table of the 63 elements known during his time. He left gaps in the periodic table to show that there were still more elements to be discovered. There are currently 118 known elements.

In the 1900s, research was being done on the structure of the atom. Niels Bohr (1885-1962) proposed the first model of the atom to incorporate quantum physics. Bohr devised the concept of having the electrons in different energy levels in an atom.

The Development of Chemistry

The term *chemistry* was used for the first time around A.D. 400–409, and it was used in reference to changing matter. Chemistry and the chemical industry really has its roots in the kitchen—pounding grain and other foods, boiling food in pots, straining to separate solids and liquids, fermentation, etc. Salt was probably one of the first chemicals used. Salt is found in the seas and inside the earth. Salt has been used for many things including flavoring and preserving foods, melting snow and ice, softening water, processing fabrics and leather, mummification, making pottery, and building churches. Salt was also used as a medicine in ointments, powders, and syrups. Another commonly used early chemical was sodium. It was used as a preservative, in glasses and glazes for pottery, and in cleaning textiles. Other early chemicals were plant and animal dyes.

Chemistry is the study of substances and how they interact with other substances. The scientific definition of chemistry is the study of the composition of matter and the changes that the matter undergoes. Chemistry is related to many areas of science including biology, geology, physiology, physics, medicine, and so on. There are many practical applications of chemistry in the world around us. Clothes are made from synthetic fibers and natural or manmade dyes. Cooking is chemistry. For example, when baking a cake, several different substances are mixed and baked, which results in a new substance.

In the 1800s, chemistry was divided into three main branches: inorganic, organic, and physical chemistry. **Inorganic chemistry** is the study of compounds without carbon. **Organic chemistry** is the study of substances containing carbon. **Physical chemistry** deals with the study of heat, electricity, and other forms of energy in chemical processes. Two more branches of chemistry were added: **analytical chemistry**, which deals with the composition of substances, and **biochemistry**, which is the study of the chemistry of living organisms.

Some of the processes used by chemists are filtration, distillation, fermentation, and sublimation. **Filtration** uses porous materials to separate solids from liquids, (i.e., a coffee filter allows the coffee oils through but not the grounds). **Distillation** is a process by which a liquid is turned into a vapor and condensed back into a liquid. This process is used to separate liquids from dissolved solids or volatile liquids from less volatile ones. For example, salt can be removed from seawater by allowing the water to evaporate and re-condense in another container. **Fermentation** is the production of alcohol from sugar through the action of yeast or bacteria. **Sublimation** is when a solid turns to a gas without first changing to a liquid (i.e., mothballs).

Introduction to the Concepts/Topic Area (cont.)

Scientific Concepts

Chemistry is the study of the structure, properties, and composition of substances and the changes to those substances (Wilbraham, Staley, Matta, Waterman, 2002). It is important to understand the basic concepts of chemistry and its application because it is a part of everyday life. Chemistry is involved in food production and preparation, making medicines, the life processes of animals and plants, safety equipment, materials production, forensic science, health and sanitation, fuels, dyes, tree color changes in the fall, home heating and cooling, and fabric and textile production. Another important reason to study chemistry is to study the impact some chemicals have on the environment and the long-term effects of certain chemicals in the environment. The study of chemistry is needed to try to change the negative effects of some of the technology and chemicals produced as by-products, such as the impact that aerosol sprays have had on the ozone layer.

States of Matter

This study of chemistry begins with an examination of matter. There are two theories about the makeup of matter, atomic and molecular. **Atomic Theory** states that matter is made up of atoms. **Molecular Theory** states that matter is made of molecules. **Matter** is defined as anything that has mass and takes up space or has volume. The second activity in this book is an air activity in which it is shown that air is matter if it has mass and takes up space. Matter has been classified into four states or phases of matter: solid, liquid, gas, and plasma. This book focuses on three of the states of matter because the concept of plasma is too abstract for students of this age.

Solids have a definite shape and volume. This means that solids keep their shape and take up the same amount of space. Solids have a high cohesive force so the molecules of solids are packed tightly together. The **cohesive force** is the attraction of like substances. Molecules are in constant motion; however, in solids, the molecules are moving so slowly you cannot see them move.

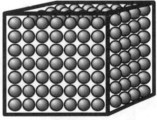

Solid

Liquids have a definite volume but no definite shape. Liquids will take up the same amount of space but will take the shape of the container in which they are placed. At the molecular level, the liquids have a low cohesive force, so the molecules of a liquid are spread far enough apart that they can flow over each other and move a little faster.

Liquid

5

Introduction to the Concepts/Topic Area (cont.)

Gases have no definite volume or shape. The cohesive force of gases is almost nonexistent, so the molecules are not attracted to each other. The gases will expand to fill any container and will take the shape of the container.

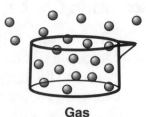

Gas

Plasma has no definite shape or volume and is a highly energized gas. As with other gases, the cohesive force of plasma is almost nonexistent, so the molecules are not attracted to each other. The gases will expand to fill any container and will take the shape of the container.

Properties of Matter

Properties of matter can be divided into two types: physical properties and chemical properties.

Physical Properties

Physical properties can be observed or measured without changing the chemical structure of the substance. Physical properties include mass, volume, and density. **Mass** is the amount of matter present, and it remains constant. The metric basic unit of measure for mass is the **gram**. **Volume** is how much space something takes up, and the basic metric unit of measure for volume is the **liter**. The volume of some objects, such as a block of wood, may be found mathematically by taking the length times the width times the height.

V = Length x Width x Height   OR   L x W x H

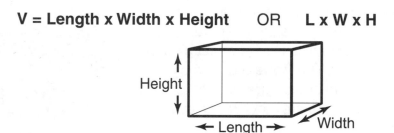

The volume of other three-dimensional objects, such as spheres and pyramids, can also be found mathematically. The volume of an irregular object, such as a rock, can be found by using a method called **displacement**. Water is added to a calibrated container, such as a measuring cup, and recorded. Once the volume of water has been recorded, the rock is added, and the level of the water is recorded again. The difference between the first measurement and the second is the volume of the rock. When reading a measuring cup or graduated cylinder, the liquid has a tendency to cling to the sides of the container, creating a curve called the **meniscus**. The tendency of unlike materials to be attracted to each other is called **adhesion**. When reading the volume, you must measure from the bottom of this curve.

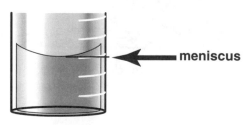

meniscus

Introduction to the Concepts/Topic Area (cont.)

Finding the Volume of Irregular Shapes By Displacement

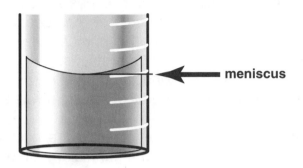 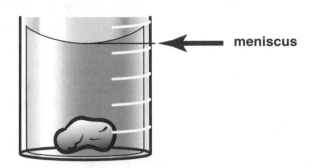

First reading: take reading from the bottom of the meniscus.

Second reading: take reading from the bottom of the meniscus.

Density is the relationship between mass and volume. It can be calculated by dividing the mass by the volume.

$$\text{Density} = \frac{\text{Mass}}{\text{Volume}} \qquad \text{OR} \qquad D = \frac{M}{V}$$

For example, the mass of 1 milliliter of water is 1 gram at 4 degrees Celsius. The density of water is calculated by:

$$D = \frac{1\,\text{gram}}{1\,\text{milliliter}} \qquad \text{OR} \qquad \text{a Density of 1g/ml}$$

Knowing the relationship of mass to volume or density will help you determine whether or not an object will sink or float.

Chemical Properties

Chemical properties allow substances to chemically react to other substances to form new substances. These changes occur at the atomic or molecular level. **Atomic Theory** states that matter is made of atoms. Atoms are the smallest part of an element and are the building blocks of all matter; they combine to form elements and molecules. Atoms consist of electrons, protons, neutrons, and hundreds of sub-atomic particles. For middle-school students, the discussion should focus on the electrons, protons, and neutrons. **Electrons** have a negative charge and circle around the nucleus of the atom. The nucleus contains protons and neutrons. **Protons** have a positive charge, and **neutrons** are neutral or have no charge. Most of the mass of an atom is from the protons and neutrons and is in the nucleus.

Models of the atom are changing as more is learned about them. John Dalton's (1766–1844) Atomic Theory stated that atoms were a solid, indivisible mass.

Introduction to the Concepts/Topic Area (cont.)

J. J. Thomson (1856–1940) discovered atoms contained electrons. He described the "plum pudding" model of an atom with charged electrons stuck into a lump of positively-charged material (i.e., a ball of peanut brittle with the candy part making up the positively-charged material and the peanuts the electrons). However, this model did not describe the number of electrons and protons, their arrangement, or that electrons could be removed to form ions.

Ernest Rutherford (1871–1937) discovered that atoms contained a nucleus. He proposed that atoms had a nucleus surrounded by electrons. He thought the rest of the atom was empty space.

Niels Bohr (1885–1962) suggested that the electrons moved around the nucleus in concentric circular paths or orbits. He further stated that electrons in a particular path have a fixed energy. In order for them to move from one orbit to another, they must gain or lose energy. A **quantum of energy** is the amount of energy needed to move an electron from its current level to the next higher level. This concept is where the term **quantum leap**, which describes an abrupt change, originates.

James Chadwick (1891–1974) discovered that the nuclei of atoms contained neutrons that carried no charge.

Erwin Schrodinger (1887–1961) used quantum theory to develop the **quantum mechanical model** of the atom. In this model, electrons have a restricted value, but they do not have a specified path around the nucleus. They are in a cloud around the nucleus.

Since the current theory of atomic structure consists of electrons, protons, neutrons, and hundreds of sub-atomic particles, Bohr's model is the easiest for students at this level to understand.

Using Bohr's Model to Represent Chadwick's Notion of the Atom - Nucleus With Positively Charged Protons and Neutrons With No Charge Surrounded by Negatively Charged Electrons Orbiting Around the Nucleus

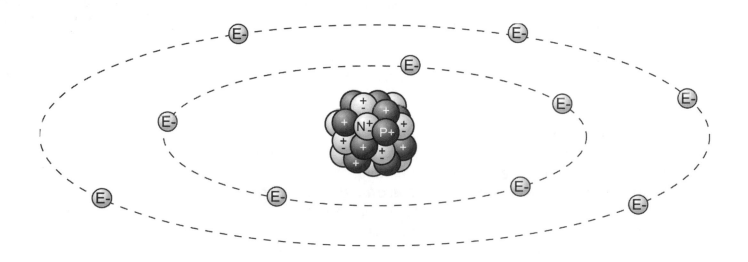

Introduction to the Concepts/Topic Area (cont.)

Elements

Elements are substances made up of only one kind of atom that cannot be divided by ordinary laboratory means. Ordinary laboratory means might include physical separation, filtration, or distillation. The **Periodic Law** states that an element's properties depend upon its atomic weight. Dimitri Mendeleev developed this discovery into the periodic table of the 63 elements known during his time. He left gaps in the periodic table showing that there were still more elements to be discovered. Currently there are 118 known elements. By organizing the elements by atomic number in the periodic table, groups of elements emerged. The horizontal rows are **periods**. The Periodic Law states that when elements are arranged by increasing atomic number, their physical and chemical properties are the same. These periods are arranged according to the atomic number, which is the number of protons in the nucleus. The columns represent **groups** or **families** that have similar physical and chemical properties.

Schrodinger - Nucleus With a Cloud of Electrons Around. Quantum Mechanical Model (Cloud Model) - Mathematical Model of Atom.

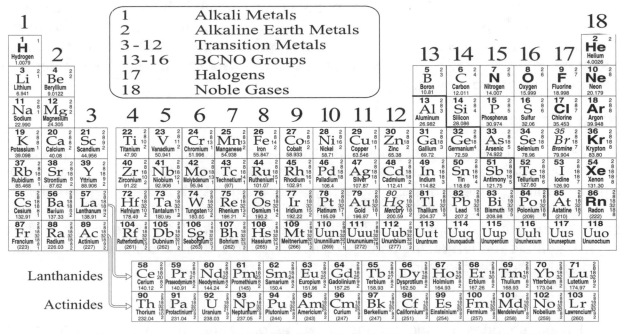

The Periodic Table of the Elements

1	Alkali Metals
2	Alkaline Earth Metals
3 - 12	Transition Metals
13-16	BCNO Groups
17	Halogens
18	Noble Gases

Liquid - Br, Hg   Gas - H, He, N, O, F, Ne, Cl, Ar, Kr, Xe, Rn   Solid - All Others

Introduction to the Concepts/Topic Area (cont.)

Each box on the periodic table has the atomic number, which represents the number of protons or positively-charged particles in the nucleus. The number of electrons always equals the number of protons in an electrically-balanced atom. Atoms of the same element have the same number of protons but may have a different number of neutrons. Elements with different numbers of neutrons are called **isotopes**. **Atomic weights** are determined by comparing the element with an atom of carbon 12, which is assigned the weight of 12 units. The **atomic mass numbers** are often used in place of atomic weights. Atomic mass is the number of protons and neutrons found in the atom.

In the Periodic Table of the Elements

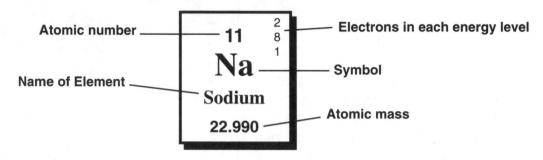

Molecules

Atoms can combine to form new substances called molecules. Chemical bonds hold the atoms of the molecule together. Molecules are in constant motion. **Molecules** are the smallest part of a compound that still has the properties of the compound. A molecule is a neutral, chemically-bonded group of atoms that acts as one unit. Molecules are in constant motion in all states of matter. Molecules of a solid are packed tightly together, have strong cohesive force, and move slowly. **Cohesion** is the attraction of like substances. Molecules of a liquid are spread farther apart and have a lower cohesive force that allows the molecules to slide over one another, and they move more rapidly. In a gas, molecules have very little cohesive force, are spread farther apart, and move very rapidly.

Changes in Matter

Matter can undergo different kinds of changes: physical, chemical, and nuclear. A **physical change** is an alteration in a substance that does not change the chemical makeup of the substance. Cutting a piece of paper is a physical change. A **chemical change** takes place when substances are combined, and they change their chemical structure. During a chemical reaction, atoms are rearranged into new substances. An animal digesting food is a chemical change. In a **nuclear change**, the change takes place in the nucleus of the atom. This happens in fusion and fission reactions in nuclear reactors.

Physical Changes

Physical changes include changes in states of matter. The states of matter are solid, liquid, gas, and plasma. Heat is added or taken away when matter changes from one state to

Introduction to the Concepts/Topic Area (cont.)

another. Evaporation, condensation, and sublimation are processes of these changes in state. **Evaporation** is the process of a liquid changing to a gas when it is heated. When alcohol is placed on your body, it has a cooling sensation because the heat in your body causes the alcohol to quickly change into a gas. **Condensation** is the process of a gas changing to a liquid when it is cooled. When warm breath comes in contact with a cold window, the water vapor in it condenses on the window. **Sublimation** occurs when a solid changes directly to a gas without changing to a liquid first. Mothballs change to a gas through the process of sublimation.

Diffusion is also a physical change. The tendency of molecules to move from an area of high concentration to low concentration is diffusion. Putting a tea bag in water is an example of diffusion. The tea bag has a high concentration of tea; the water has a low concentration. The tea molecules then have a tendency to move into the water until there is an equal concentration in each. The temperature of the water determines how fast the diffusion takes place. Heat is also being exchanged in this action. Some of the heat from the water is being transferred to the tea in the tea bag. Heat can be transferred through conduction, convection, or radiation. **Conduction** is when heat is transferred by collisions of the particles of the substance. **Convection** is when heat energy is transferred in gas or liquid by the currents in the heated fluid. In **radiation**, energy is transferred by electromagnetic waves.

A **mixture** is made when two or more substances are physically combined but not chemically joined together. The substances still have the same properties as before they were combined and can be separated by ordinary physical means. Mixing table salt in water is an example of a mixture. The table salt dissolves in the water and seems to disappear. However, the table salt molecules actually take up the spaces between the water molecules. When the water is evaporated, the salt will remain. The table salt and water do not lose their own properties.

Other physical characteristics of matter include adhesion and cohesion. **Adhesion** is the attraction between unlike substances. Adhesion is why water and nutrients rise in plant stems. This concept explains why colored water seems to climb up a paper towel. **Cohesion** is the attraction of like substances. Cohesive forces allow you to add more water to a glass that is level full and make a dome of water on top. It is also the reason three streams of water merge into one stream when they are close together.

Chemical Changes

Matter can also change chemically. This change happens at the atomic level. A compound has two or more substances that are chemically combined to form a new substance. The structures of each of the substances change at the atomic level. This means they can only be separated by another chemical reaction. An example of a chemical compound is water. Water is made of hydrogen and oxygen; both are invisible gases at room temperature before they are combined. After they are combined, they form water, a clear liquid at room temperature.

Chemical reactions can happen spontaneously, or they may need some form of energy. Heat, light, mechanical devices, and catalysts provide energy for some chemical reactions. Some chemical reactions happen immediately while others happen over time. Adding catalysts, increasing the surface area, increasing concentration, and heating are used to speed up reactions. How well these chemical changes occur is determined by how strongly the electrons are held in the outer shells of the atom.

Introduction to the Concepts/Topic Area (cont.)

Fire or burning is a chemical reaction. It is the process of the fuel combining rapidly with oxygen. This process is call **rapid oxidation**. Decaying plant matter, such as grass clippings in a garbage bag, will become warm, showing a chemical reaction is taking place. In this process, the materials slowly combine with oxygen for **slow oxidation**.

A precipitate is one indicator of a chemical change. A **precipitate** is an insoluble substance created during the reaction that settles out as a solid in the bottom of the container. Changes in temperature or color are indicators that something has changed chemically. During a chemical reaction, heat may be given off or absorbed. If the heat is absorbed, it is an **endothermic reaction**; if it is given off, it is an **exothermic reaction**. If the substances give off an odor or gas, it is also an indication of a chemical change.

Acids are substances that produce or donate hydrogen ions in a solution. **Bases** produce hydroxide ions or accept hydrogen ions in solution. **Salts** are formed when acids are combined with bases or metals. When they react, they make water plus a salt. Acids and bases can be detected by using red and blue litmus paper. Red litmus paper turns blue, indicating a base. Blue litmus paper turns red when an acid is present. The strength of the acid or base can be determined by using pH paper. Strong acids, such as sulfuric or

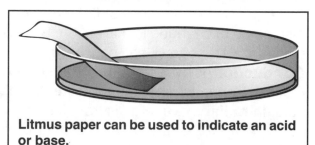

Litmus paper can be used to indicate an acid or base.

hydrochloric acid, have a pH of 1. Milder acids, such as citrus fruits and vinegar, have a pH of 4. Water usually has the pH of 6–7. This pH is neutral; however, there may be variations in the water due to the water purification processes used in the area. Soaps are formed by the reaction of organic acids with a strong base, and they are mildly basic with a pH of 8–9. Strong bases, such as oven cleaners that contain lye, have a pH of 10. A simple indicator to use in determining the pH of a substance is purple cabbage juice. In the presence of an acid, the cabbage juice turns pink. Bases turn the purple juice green, and neutral substances do not change the color.

Nuclear Changes

The third type of changes are nuclear changes. **Nuclear changes** occur within the nucleus of the atom. **Fission** is the process of splitting the nucleus of the atom apart. **Fusion** occurs when the nuclei of two or more atoms join together. Both fission and fusion release tremendous amounts of energy.

NOTE: Goggles are recommended when dealing with any kind of chemicals or other eye hazards.

Naive Concepts

Naive ideas related to chemistry:

- Gases are invisible and are not matter.
- Gases do not have mass.
- A thick liquid has a higher density than water.
- Mass and volume are the same property.
- Air and oxygen are the same gas.
- Expansion of matter is due to the expansion of particles rather than to increased particle spacing.
- Particles of solids have no motion.
- Relative particle spacing among solids, liquids, and gases (1:1:10) is incorrectly perceived and not generally related to the density of the states.
- Materials can only exhibit properties of one state of matter.
- Melting/freezing and boiling/condensation are often understood only in terms of water.
- There is no difference between atoms and molecules.
- Chemical changes are perceived as additive, rather than interactive. After chemical changes, the original substances are perceived as remaining, even though they are altered.
- Formation of a new substance with new properties is seen as a simple happening, rather than as the result of particle rearrangement. (American Institute of Physics, 2000)
- Salt only refers to common table salt.

Definitions of Terms

Chemistry is the study of the structure, properties, and composition of substances and the changes to the substances. (Hewitt, 2002)

Matter is anything that takes up space or has mass.

Matter has been classified into four states or forms of matter: solid, liquid, gas, and plasma. This book focuses on three of these states of matter because plasma is too abstract a concept for students of this age to grasp.

Solids have a definite shape and volume. This means that solids keep their shape and take up the same amount of space. At the molecular level, the molecules of solids are packed tightly together and are moving so slowly you cannot see them move. Solids have a high cohesive force.

Liquids have a definite volume but no definite shape. This means liquids will take up the same amount of space but will take the shape of the container in which they are placed. At the molecular level, the molecules of a liquid are spread far enough apart that they can flow over each other, and move a little faster than in a solid. Liquids have a low cohesive force.

Definitions of Terms (cont.)

Gases have no definite volume or shape. This means gases will expand to fill any container and will take the shape of the container. The cohesive force of gases is almost nonexistent.

Plasma has no definite shape or volume and is a highly energized gas.

Physical Properties of Matter:

Physical properties of matter include mass, volume, and density.

Mass is the amount of matter present.

Volume is the amount of space something takes up.

Density is the mass per unit volume. At the molecular level, it is how closely the molecules are packed together in a specific area. It can be determined by dividing the mass by the volume.

Archimedes' Principle states that an object placed in a liquid seems to lose an amount of weight equal to the amount of fluid it displaces.

Chemical Properties of Matter:

Chemical properties of matter are related to the atoms and molecules of the substance.

Atoms are the smallest part of an element. Atoms consist of electrons, protons, neutrons, and hundreds of sub-atomic particles.

Elements are substances made up of only one kind of atom that cannot be divided by ordinary chemical means.

Molecules are the smallest part of a compound that still has the properties of the compound. Molecules are in constant motion in all states of matter.

Atomic Theory states that matter is made up of atoms.

Molecular Theory states that matter is made up of molecules.

Adhesion is the attraction between unlike substances. Adhesion is why water and nutrients rise in plant stems.

Definitions of Terms (cont.)

Cohesion is the attraction of like substances. Cohesive forces allow you to add more water to a glass that is level full and make a dome of water on top. It is also the reason three streams of water merge into one stream when they are close together.

The Law of Conservation of Matter states that matter cannot be created or destroyed.

Changes in matter can be physical or chemical changes.

Physical Changes:

Physical changes in matter include adding or taking away heat energy to change states; evaporation, condensation, and sublimation; diffusion; conduction, convection, and radiation.

Adding or taking away heat changes matter from one state to the other. For example, adding heat to a solid changes it to a liquid. Taking away heat changes a liquid to a solid or a gas to a liquid in most cases.

Evaporation occurs when a substance is changed from a liquid to a gas. For example, water is turned into steam when it boils, or water turns to vapor when the sun shines on a body of water.

Condensation occurs when a substance turns from a gas to a liquid. (i.e., when warm breath comes into contact with a cold window, the water turns to liquid; or while an ice-cold drink is sitting in the warm moist air, the moisture condenses on the cold surface of the container).

Sublimation is when a substance changes directly from a solid to a gas without first changing to a liquid. An example of this is mothballs.

Diffusion happens when a substance moves from an area of higher concentration to an area of lower concentration. An example of this is tea in a tea bag. The tea in the bag is the area of higher concentration, and it flows into the water which is an area of lower concentration of tea.

Mixtures are formed when two or more substances are mixed but are not chemically combined. They can be separated by ordinary physical means.

Solutions are formed when substances dissolve in a solid or liquid. Sugar or salt can be dissolved in water to form a solution.

A **colloid** is formed when larger particles of matter are suspended in a solid, liquid, or gas.

Conduction occurs when heat is transferred by collisions of the particles of the substance.

Convection occurs when heat is transferred into gas or liquid by the currents in the heated fluid.

Definitions of Terms (cont.)

In **radiation**, energy is transferred by electromagnetic waves.

Chemical Changes:

When a **chemical change** takes place, a new substance with new properties is formed.

Compounds are formed during a chemical change. They are substances that can only be separated into simpler substances by a chemical reaction.

Acids are compounds that produce hydrogen ions in solutions.

Bases are compounds that produce hydroxide ions in solution.

When acids and bases are combined, they form water and some kind of salt.

Salts are formed when acids and bases are combined.

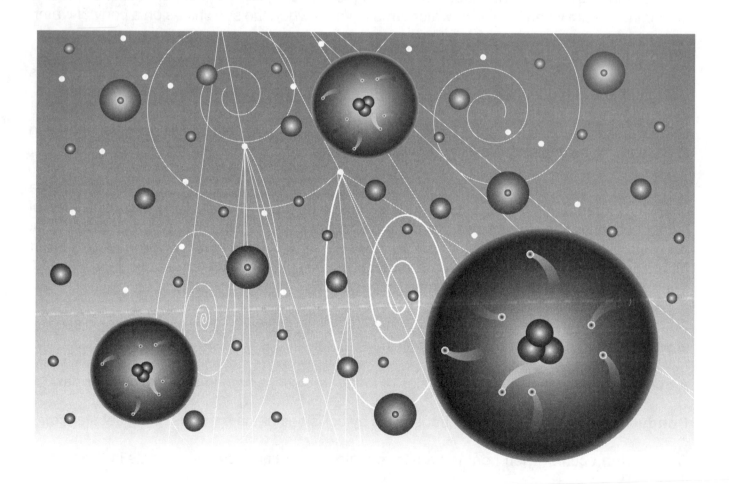

National Standards Related to Chemistry

National Science Education Standards (NSES) Content Standards (NRC, 1996)
National Research Council (1996). *National Science Education Standards.* Washington, D.C.:
    National Academy Press.

Unifying Concepts K-12
Systems, order, and organization
Evidence, models, and explanation
Change, constancy, and measurement
Form and function

NSES Content Standard A: Inquiry
- Abilities necessary to do scientific inquiry
- Understanding about inquiry

NSES Content Standard B: 5-8 Properties and Changes of Properties in Matter
- A substance has characteristic properties—density, boiling point, solubility. A mixture can often be separated into original substances.
- Substances react chemically in characteristic ways with other substances to form new substances with different properties; conservation of mass in chemical reactions; substances are grouped if they react in similar ways.
- Chemical elements do not break down by ordinary chemical laboratory treatments, such as heating, exposure to electric current, or reaction with acids. There are over 100 known elements that combine to form compounds (NRC, 1996).

NSES Content Standard B: 5-8 Transfer of Energy
- Energy is a property of many substances and is associated with heat, light, electricity, mechanical motion, sound, nuclei, and the nature of a chemical; energy is transferred in many ways.
- Electrical circuits provide a means of transferring electrical energy when heat, light, sound, and chemical changes are produced.
- In most chemical and nuclear reactions, energy is transferred into or out of the system; heat, light, mechanical motion, or electricity might be involved (NRC, 1996).

NSES Content Standard C: Life Science 5-8
- Structure and function in living systems

NSES Content Standard D: Earth and Space
- Structure of the earth system

NSES Content Standard E: Science and Technology 5-8
- Abilities of technological design
- Understanding about science and technology

National Standards Related to Chemistry (cont.)

NSES Content Standard F: Science in Personal and Social Perspectives 5-8
- Personal health
- Science and technology in society

NSES Content Standard G: History and Nature of Science 5-8
- Science as a human endeavor
- Nature of science
- History of science

Principles And Standards For School Mathematics (NCTM, 2000)
National Council for Teachers of Mathematics. (2000). *Principles and Standards for School Mathematics.* Reston, VA: National Council for Teachers of Mathematics.

Number and Operations
- Understand numbers, ways of representing numbers, relationships among numbers, and number systems.
- Understand meanings of operations and how they relate to one another.
- Compute fluently and make reasonable estimates.

Algebra
- Understand patterns, relations, and functions.
- Represent and analyze mathematical situations and structures using algebraic symbols.
- Use mathematical models to represent and understand quantitative relationships.
- Analyze change in various contexts.

Geometry
- Analyze characteristics and properties of two- and three-dimensional geometric shapes and develop mathematical arguments about geometric relationships.
- Specify locations and describe spatial relationships using coordinate geometry and other representational systems.
- Apply transformations and use symmetry to analyze mathematical situations.
- Use visualization, spatial reasoning, and geometric modeling to solve problems.

Measurement
- Understand measurable attributes of objects and the units, systems, and processes of measurement.
- Apply appropriate techniques, tools, and formulas to determine measurements.

Data Analysis and Probability
- Formulate questions that can be addressed with data, and collect, organize, and display relevant data to answer them.
- Select and use appropriate statistical methods to analyze data.
- Develop and evaluate inferences and predictions that are based on data.
- Understand and apply basic concepts of probability.

Science Process Skills: Chemistry

Introduction: Science is organized curiosity, and an important part of this organization is the thinking skills or information processing skills. We ask the question "Why?" and then must plan a strategy for answering the question or questions. In the process of answering our questions, we make and carefully record observations, make predictions, identify and control variables, measure, make inferences, and communicate our findings. Additional skills may be called upon depending on the nature of our questions. In this way, science is a verb involving active manipulation of materials and careful thinking. Science is dependent upon language, math, and reading skills as well as the specialized thinking skills associated with identifying and solving problems.

BASIC PROCESS SKILLS

Classifying: Grouping, ordering, arranging, or distributing objects, events, or information into categories based on properties or criteria, according to some method or system.

> Example – The skill is being demonstrated if the student is …
> Grouping substances by their physical properties into categories. These categories might include states of matter, such as solids, liquids, and gases; or elements, compounds, or mixtures.

Observing: Using the senses (or extensions of the senses) to gather information about an object or event.

> Example – The skill is being demonstrated if the student is …
> Seeing and describing the physical or chemical properties of a substance.

Measuring: Using both standard and nonstandard measures or estimates to describe the dimensions of an object or event. Making quantitative observations.

> Example – The skill is being demonstrated if the student is …
> Using a graduated cylinder to measure the volume of a liquid or an irregularly shaped object or using a ruler to measure the volume of a block.

Inferring: Making an interpretation or conclusion based on reasoning to explain an observation.

> Example – The skill is being demonstrated if the student is…
> Stating that a chemical change has taken place by observations or tests conducted on the new substance.

Communicating: Communicating ideas through speaking or writing. Students may share the results of investigations, collaborate on solving problems, and gather and interpret data both orally and in writing. Uses graphs, charts, and diagrams to describe data.

Science Process Skills: Chemistry (cont.)

> Example – The skill is being demonstrated if the student is …
> Describing an event or a set of observations. Participating in brainstorming and hypothesizing before an investigation. Formulating initial and follow-up questions in the study of a topic. Summarizing data, interpreting findings, and offering conclusions. Questioning or refuting previous findings. Making decisions or using a graph to show the relationship between temperature and the decrease in size of a melting ice cube over time.

Predicting: Making a forecast of future events or conditions in the context of previous observations and experiences.

> Example – The skill is being demonstrated if the student is …
> Stating how fast an ice cube will melt at a specific temperature based on data collected through experimentation and observation.

Manipulating Materials: Handling or treating materials and equipment skillfully and effectively.

> Example – The skill is being demonstrated if the student is …
> Arranging equipment and materials needed to conduct an investigation; and setting up and conducting an experiment to determine air is matter by showing that it has mass and takes up space.

Replicating: Performing acts that duplicate demonstrated symbols, patterns, or procedures.

> Example – The skill is being demonstrated if the student is …
> Using a double-pan balance following procedures previously demonstrated or modeled by another person or following a procedure to set up a double-pan balance made from common materials.

Using Numbers: Applying mathematical rules or formulas to calculate quantities or determine relationships from basic measurements.

> Example – The skill is being demonstrated if the student is …
> Computing the density of a substance using the formula **Density = Mass divided by Volume**.

Developing Vocabulary: Specialized terminology and unique uses of common words in relation to a given topic need to be identified and given meaning.

> Example – The skill is being demonstrated if the student is …
> Using context clues, working definitions, glossaries or dictionaries, word structure (roots, prefixes, suffixes), and synonyms and antonyms to clarify meaning.

Science Process Skills: Chemistry (cont.)

Questioning: Questions serve to focus inquiry, determine prior knowledge, and establish purposes or expectations for an investigation. An active search for information is promoted when questions are used.

> Example – The skill is being demonstrated if the student is ...
> Using what is already known about a topic or concept to formulate questions for further investigation; hypothesizing and predicting prior to gathering data; or formulating questions as new information is acquired.

Using Cues: Key words and symbols convey significant meaning in messages. Organizational patterns facilitate comprehension of major ideas. Graphic features clarify textual information.

> Example – The skill is being demonstrated if the student is ...
> Listing or underlining words and phrases that carry the most important details or relating key words together to express a main idea or concept.

INTEGRATED PROCESS SKILLS

Creating Models: Displaying information by means of graphic illustrations or other multisensory representations.

> Example – The skill is being demonstrated if the student is ...
> Drawing a graph or diagram; constructing a three-dimensional object, using a digital camera to record an event, constructing a chart or table, or producing a picture or diagram that illustrates information about the molecular structures of the states of matter.

Formulating Hypotheses: Stating or constructing a statement that is testable about what is thought to be the expected outcome of an experiment (based on reasoning).

> Example – The skill is being demonstrated if the student is ...
> Making a statement to be used as the basis for an experiment, i.e., If heat is added or taken away, matter changes from one state to another.

Generalizing: Drawing general conclusions from particulars.

> Example – The skill is being demonstrated if the student is ...
> Making a summary statement following analysis of experimental results, i.e., Matter changes from a solid to a liquid by adding heat.

Science Process Skills: Chemistry (cont.)

Identifying and Controlling Variables: Recognizing the characteristics of objects or factors in events that are constant or change under different conditions and that can affect an experimental outcome, keeping most variables constant while manipulating only one variable.

> Example – The skill is being demonstrated if the student is …
> Listing or describing the factors that would influence the outcome of an experiment, such as the temperature and humidity of the air during an evaporation experiment.

Defining Operationally: Stating how to measure a variable in an experiment, defining a variable according to the actions or operations to be performed on or with it.

> Example – The skill is being demonstrated if the student is …
> Defining such things as heat in the context of materials and actions for a specific activity. Heat energy gain or loss can be measured by the increase or decrease in temperature.

Recording and Interpreting Data: Collecting bits of information about objects and events, which illustrate a specific situation; organizing and analyzing data that has been obtained; and drawing conclusions from it by determining apparent patterns or relationships in the data.

> Example – The skill is being demonstrated if the student is …
> Recording data (taking notes, making lists/outlines, recording numbers on charts/graphs, making tape recordings, taking photographs, writing numbers of results of observations/ measurements) from the series of experiments to determine if air is matter and forming a conclusion that relates trends in data to variables.

Making Decisions: Identifying alternatives and choosing a course of action from among alternatives after basing the judgment for the selection on justifiable reasons.

> Example – The skill is being demonstrated if the student is …
> Identifying alternative ways to solve a problem through the use of physical or chemical properties of a substance; analyzing the consequences of each alternative, such as cost, the effect on other people or the environment; using justifiable reasons as the basis for making choices; and choosing freely from the alternatives.

Experimenting: Being able to conduct an experiment, including asking an appropriate question, stating a hypothesis, identifying and controlling variables, operationally defining those variables, designing a "fair" experiment, and interpreting the results of an experiment.

> Example – The skill is being demonstrated if the student is …
> Utilizing the entire process of designing, building, and testing various substances to solve a problem. Arranging equipment and materials to conduct an investigation, manipulating the equipment and materials, and conducting the investigation. An experiment was designed and conducted in the "Is Air Matter?" activity.

Name: _____ Date: _____

Student Inquiry Activity 1: Matter—What Is Matter?

Topic: What is matter? What are the properties of matter?

Standards:
NSES Unifying Concepts and Processes, (A), (B), (C), (D), (E), (F), (G)
NCTM Data Analysis and Probability, Measurement, Geometry
See **National Standards Section** for more information on each standard.

Naive Concepts:
Gases are invisible and are not matter.
Gases do not have mass.
Air and oxygen are the same gas.
Formation of a new substance with new properties is seen as a simple happening rather than as the result of particle rearrangement. (American Institute of Physics, 2000).

Materials:
A variety of substances found around the house, such as:

Balloon filled with your breath	Grocery bag filled with air
Block of wood	Furniture
Water	Soft drink
Leaf, twig, plant, etc.	Feather
Book	Milk
Juice	Paste/glue
Silverware	Rocks

Goggles are recommended.

Science Skills:
    Observations will be made about materials or substances found around the house. The substances used will be **classified** into groups based on their common properties. The substances will be **manipulated** during the examination to determine their physical characteristics. Findings will be **communicated** through **data collection** and **writing conclusions**. Through this activity, student will develop **vocabulary** related to chemistry. **Data** will be **recorded and interpreted** to identify possible groups for your substances.

Content Background:
    There are two theories about the makeup of matter—atomic and molecular. **Atomic theory** states that matter is made up of atoms. **Molecular theory** states that matter is made up of molecules. Matter is defined as anything that has mass and takes up space or has volume. Matter has been classified into four states or phases of matter: solid, liquid, gas, and plasma. This book focuses on three of these states of matter because the concept of plasma is too abstract of a subject for students of this age. This study of chemistry begins with an examination of matter.
    Solids have a definite shape and volume. This means that solids keep their shape and take up the same amount of space. Solids have a high cohesive force, so the molecules of

Student Inquiry Activity **1**: Matter—What Is Matter? (cont.)

solids are packed tightly together. The cohesive force is the attraction of like substances. Molecules are in constant motion; however, in solids, the molecules are moving so slowly you cannot see them move.

Liquids have a definite volume but no definite shape. Liquids will take up the same amount of space but will take the shape of the container in which they are placed. At the molecular level, the liquids have a low cohesive force, so the molecules of a liquid are spread far enough apart that they can flow over each other, and move a little faster than in a solid.

Gases have no definite volume or shape. The cohesive force of gases is almost nonexistent, so the molecules are not attracted to each other. A gas will expand to fill any container and will take the shape of the container.

Plasma has no definite shape or volume and is a highly energized gas. As with other gases, the cohesive force of plasma is almost nonexistent, so the molecules are not attracted to each other. The plasma will expand to fill any container and will take the shape of the container.

Properties of Matter can be divided into two types—physical properties and chemical properties. **Physical properties** can be observed or measured without changing the chemical structure of the substance. These include the mass, volume, and density. **Chemical properties** allow substances to chemically react to other substances to form new substances. These changes occur at the atomic or molecular level. This activity focuses on physical properties.

Challenge Question: What is matter?

Procedure:
1. Gather a variety of substances found around the house. (See recommended list.)
2. Carefully examine each substance.
3. Record the physical characteristics of each substance in the following chart. How are they alike? How are they different?

Substance	Physical Characteristics

Name: _____ Date: _____

Student Inquiry Activity 1: Matter—What Is Matter? (cont.)

Substance	Physical Characteristics

Exploration/ Data Collection:

1. Determine one physical characteristic with which you could group the substances with similar properties.

Substance	Group

2. Describe the characteristics used to group the substances.

_____

_____

_____

_____

_____

_____

_____

Student Inquiry Activity **1**: Matter—What Is Matter? (cont.)

Summary:

These common household substances may be classified into three categories: solids liquids, and gases. This, as the introductory activity for chemistry, begins to develop a definition and classification of matter into three of the four states of matter based on their physical properties.

Real-World Application:

All substances are made of matter and can be classified into solids, liquids, gases, and plasma. Solids, liquids, and gases will be covered in this book.

Extensions:

Go on a field trip and try to identify other substances that will fit into the categories of solids, liquids, and gases.

Activity One Assessment:

Use the following guidelines to assess student performance in this activity. Check those statements that apply.

Observations of Substances

_____ Physical properties of the substances were identified, and detailed descriptions of the characteristics of each substance were given.

_____ Physical properties of the substances were identified with no descriptions of substance.

_____ Physical properties were not identified.

Classification of Substances

_____ Grouped all substances according to similar physical properties and was able to explain why substances were grouped the way they were.

_____ Grouped all substances according to similar physical properties.

_____ Did not group substances according to similar physical properties.

Name: _____   Date: _____

Student Inquiry Activity **2** : Matter—Is Air Matter?

Topic: Chemistry—Properties of Matter

Standards:
NSES Unifying Concepts and Processes, (A), (B), (C), (D), (E), (F), (G)
NCTM Data Analysis and Probability, Measurement, Geometry
See **National Standards Section** for more information on each standard.

Naive Concepts:

Gases are invisible and are not matter.
Gases do not have mass.
Air and oxygen are the same gas.
Formation of a new substance with new properties is seen as a simple happening rather than as the result of particle rearrangement. (American Institute of Physics, 2000)

Materials:

Plastic grocery bags (Be sure they have no holes or that the holes are taped.)
Tape
Paper clips
Masses (washers)
Goggles are recommended.

Balance - See illustrations for assembly.
Tape
String
Ruler
Pencil
Cup
Paper clips

OR

Pegboard™
String
Ruler
Pencil
Cup
Paper clips
Broom handle
Wooden base

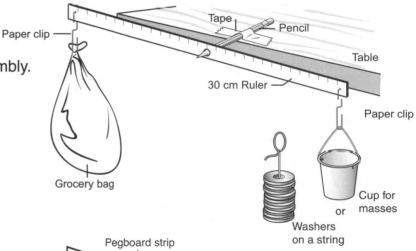

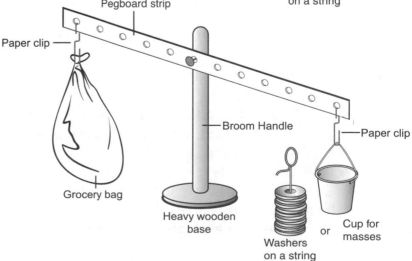

Student Inquiry Activity 2 : Matter—Is Air Matter? (cont.)

Science Skills:

You will make **observations** about the properties of air and will **predict** and make **inferences** as to whether or not air is matter; **classify** what state of matter air is. You will be **manipulating** the bag, masses, and balance to **use numbers to measure** the mass of a plastic bag and air. In the conclusion section, you will be **communicating** your findings. Through this activity, you will be developing **vocabulary**. You will be required to **identify and control variables**, which might affect differences in the mass recorded; **record** the mass of the bag and air; and **interpret the data** collected to determine whether or not air is matter.

Content Background:

Two theories about the makeup of matter are atomic and molecular. **Atomic Theory** states that matter is made up of atoms. **Molecular Theory** states that matter is made up of molecules. **Matter** is defined as anything that has mass and takes up space or has volume. This activity is an air activity; you can prove air is matter if you can show that it has mass and takes up space. Matter has been classified into four states or phases of matter: solid, liquid, gas, and plasma. This book focuses on three of the states of matter because the concept of plasma is too abstract for students of this age.

Gases have no definite volume or shape. The cohesive force of gases is almost nonexistent, so the molecules are not attracted to each other. The gases will expand to fill any container and will take the shape of the container.

Properties of Matter can be divided into types—physical properties and chemical properties. **Physical properties** can be observed or measured without changing the chemical structure of the substance. These include the mass, volume, and density. **Chemical properties** allow substances to chemically react to other substances to form new substances. These changes occur at the atomic or molecular level.

Physical properties of matter such as mass, volume, and density can be measured and observed. **Mass** is the amount of matter present, and it remains constant. Mass can be measured with a balance. The metric basic unit of measure for mass is the **gram**. **Volume** is how much space something takes up, and the basic metric unit of measure for volume is the **liter**. The volume of some objects, such as a block of wood, may be found mathematically by taking the length times the width times the height.

$$V = \text{Length x Width x Height} \quad \text{OR} \quad L \times W \times H$$

The volume of other three-dimensional objects, such as spheres and pyramids, can also be found mathematically. The volume of an irregular object, such as a rock, can be found by using a method called **displacement**. Water is added to a calibrated container such as a measuring cup, and recorded. When reading a measuring cup or graduated cylinder, the liquid has a tendency to cling to the sides of the container, creating a curve called the **meniscus**. The tendency of unlike materials to be attracted to each other is called **adhesion**. When reading the volume, you must measure from the bottom of this curve. Once the volume of water has been recorded, the rock is added and the level of the water is recorded again. The difference between the second measurement and the first is the volume of the rock.

Name: _____ Date: _____

Student Inquiry Activity 2 : Matter—Is Air Matter? (cont.)

Challenge Question:
Is air matter?

Hypothesis:
A hypothesis is a statement of a proposed explanation of the results.

1. State your hypothesis.

    Air is matter if _____

    _____

    _____

    _____

Procedure:
Matter is anything that has mass and takes up space.

Materials:
Plastic grocery bags. (Be sure they have no holes or that the holes are taped.)
Tape
Paper clips
Masses - small washers (outside diameter 7/8 inch (2.2 cm), inside hole diameter 3/8 inch (1 cm). Three of these small washers weigh approximately 1 gram. A nickel weighs approximately 5 grams.
Balance
Goggles are recommended.

Washer

1. Using the materials listed, design and conduct an experiment to determine if air is matter.
2. On your own paper, write out the procedure for your investigation.
3. Simple balances can be constructed as pictured on page 27.

Exploration/Data Collection:
1. Once you have determined your procedure, conduct an experiment to test your ideas.
2. Record your results in a data table.

Conclusions:
1. Does air have mass? How do you know? _____

    _____

    _____

    _____

    _____

Name: _____ Date: _____

Student Inquiry Activity **2** : Matter—Is Air Matter? (cont.)

2. Does air take up space? How do you know? _____

_____

_____

_____

_____

3. Is air matter? How do you know? _____

_____

_____

_____

_____

Summary:

Air is a gas. Matter is defined as anything that takes up space and has mass. If air takes up space and has mass, it can be inferred that it is matter. The mass of the bag before it is filled with air must be determined. Dragging the bag through the air fills it with air. (*Note: If the bag is blown up like a balloon, it will NOT be filled with air. Since human breath is mostly carbon dioxide, when the bag is filled, it is actually filled with mostly carbon dioxide. Carbon dioxide is heavier (has more mass) than air.*) The mass of the air and bag is found by subtracting the mass of the bag from the mass of the air and the bag. The difference is the mass of the air in the bag. The air has mass, which is the first part of the proof that is needed. The bag inflates, showing that air takes up space.

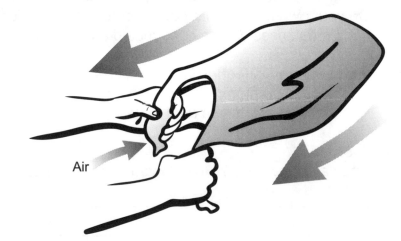

Air

Name: _____ Date: _____

Student Inquiry Activity 2 : Matter—Is Air Matter? (cont.)

Real-World Application:

Air pressure is caused by the mass of the air. Air pressure at higher altitudes is less than it is at lower altitudes. This affects the boiling point of water. Recipes must be adapted to compensate for the change in air pressure at different altitudes.

Integration:

This activity can be integrated into other science content areas such as meteorology, aerodynamics, and flight.

Extensions:

Using a rectangular tub and water, determine the amount of space the air takes up or volume by displacement. The volume of water can be determined by using the mathematical formula for volume. The volume of air and the bag can be determined by finding the volume of the water displaced by the bag filled with air. See the Volume Section in the Content Background section.

Activity Two Assessment:

Use the following guidelines to assess student performance in this activity. Check those statements that apply.

Designing and Conducting an Investigation

_____ Designed and conducted an investigation using the materials given to determine if air was matter including: identification of and controlling variables, collecting and recording data, analyzing data to draw conclusion that air is matter because it has mass and takes up space based on the evidence in the data collected.

_____ Designed and conducted an investigation using the materials given to determine if air was matter including: identification of and controlling variables, collecting and recording data, analyzing data to draw conclusions.

_____ Designed and conducted an investigation using the materials given to determine if air was matter including: identification of and controlling variables and collecting and recording data.

Name: _____ Date: _____

Student Inquiry Activity 3: People Matter—Moving Into a New State

Topic: Chemistry—States of Matter: Molecular Theory

Standards:
> **NSES** Unifying Concepts and Processes, (A), (B)
> **NCTM** Geometry

Naive Concepts:
Expansion of matter is due to the expansion of particles rather than to increased particle spacing.
Particles of solids have no motion.
Relative particle spacing among solids, liquids, and gases (1:1:10) is incorrectly perceived and not generally related to the density of the states.
Materials can only exhibit properties of one state of matter.
Melting/freezing and boiling/condensation are often understood only in terms of water.
There is no difference between atoms and molecules.

Materials:
3–8 people

Science Skills:
Students will be **inferring** the molecular structure of each of the states of matter to **create molecular models** of solids, liquids, and gases, **using the cues given** in the descriptions of each state of matter. They will be **manipulating materials** given to create the models.

Content Background:
Chemistry is the study of the structure, properties, and composition of substances and the changes to those substances (Wilbraham, Staley, Matta, Waterman, 2002). It is important to understand basic concepts of chemistry and its application because it is a part of everyday life. Chemistry is involved in food preparation and production, making medicines, the life processes of animals and plants, safety equipment, materials production, forensic science, health and sanitation, fuels, dyes, tree color changes in the fall, home heating and cooling, and fabric and textile production. Another important reason to study chemistry is to study the impact some chemicals have on the environment and the long-term effects of certain chemicals on the environment. The study of chemistry is needed to try to change the negative effects of some of the technology and chemicals produced as by-products, such as the impact that aerosol sprays have had on the ozone layer.

This study of chemistry begins with an examination of matter. There are two theories about the makeup of matter—atomic and molecular. **Atomic Theory** states that matter is made up of atoms. **Molecular Theory** states that matter is made up of molecules. **Matter** is defined as anything that has mass and takes up space or has volume. Matter has been classified into four states or phases of matter: solid, liquid, gas, and plasma. This book focuses on three of

Name: _____ Date: _____

Student Inquiry Activity 3 : People Matter—Moving Into a New State (cont.)

these states of matter because the concept of plasma is too abstract for students of this age.

Solids have a definite shape and volume. This means that solids keep their shape and take up the same amount of space. Solids have a high cohesive force, so the molecules of solids are packed tightly together. The cohesive force is the attraction of like substances. Molecules are in constant motion; however, in solids, the molecules are moving so slowly you cannot see them move.

Liquids have a definite volume but no definite shape. Liquids will take up the same amount of space but will take the shape of the container in which they are placed. At the molecular level, the liquids have a low cohesive force, so the molecules of a liquid are spread far enough apart that they can flow over each other and can move a little faster than in solids.

Gases have no definite volume or shape. The cohesive force of gases is almost nonexistent, so the molecules are not attracted to each other. The gases will expand to fill any container and will take the shape of the container.

Plasma has no definite shape or volume and is a highly energized gas. The cohesive force of plasma is almost nonexistent, so the molecules are not attracted to each other. The gases will expand to fill any container and will take the shape of the container.

Challenge Question:
What are the characteristics of each of the states of matter on the molecular level?

Procedure:
1. Find 3–8 people to help with this investigation and one or two others to make observations
2. Identify the characteristics of solids, liquids, and gases.
3. Using the people in your group, design and construct human models for a solid, a liquid, and a gas.
4. Make a drawing of each of your models.
5. On your own paper, describe how you made them and why you made them that way.

Exploration/Data Collection:

State of Matter	Characteristics
Solid	
Liquid	
Gas	

Name: _____   Date: _____

Student Inquiry Activity 3 : People Matter—Moving Into a New State (cont.)

Summary:

Solids have a definite shape and volume. This means that solids keep their shape and take up the same amount of space. Solids have a high cohesive force, so the molecules of solids are packed tightly together. The cohesive force is the attraction of like substances. Molecules are in constant motion; however, in solids, the molecules are moving so slowly you cannot see them move. The model for this state should have the people grouped tightly together but still moving.

Liquids have a definite volume but no definite shape. Liquids will take up the same amount of space but will take the shape of the container in which they are placed. At the molecular level, the liquids have a low cohesive force, so the molecules of a liquid are spread far enough apart that they can flow over each other and move a little faster than in a solid. The model for this state should have the people spread farther apart and moving more.

Gases have no definite volume or shape. The cohesive force of gases is almost nonexistent, so the molecules are not attracted to each other. The gases will expand to fill any container and will take the shape of the container. The model for this state should have the people spread all over the room and moving faster.

Solid

Liquid

Gas

Plasma has no definite shape or volume and is a highly energized gas. The cohesive force of plasma is almost nonexistent, so the molecules are not attracted to each other. The gases will expand to fill any container and will take the shape of the container. This concept is too advanced for this level, so there was no model created for this state.

Integration:

Dance or drama.

Extensions:

Design and construct models from spaghetti and marshmallows for each of the states of matter using the materials provided. Make a drawing of each of your models. Describe how you made them and why you made them that way.

Name: _____ Date: _____

Student Inquiry Activity 4 : Making Waves

Topic: Chemistry—Liquid Density

Standards:
   NSES Unifying Concepts (A), (B), (E)
   NCTM Number and Operations, Measurement, Data Analysis and Probability

---

Naive Concepts:
   A thick liquid has a higher density than water.
   Mass and volume are the same property.
   Expansion of matter is due to expansion of particles rather than to increased particle spacing.
   Relative particle spacing among solids, liquids, and gases (1:1:10) is incorrectly perceived
   and not generally related to the density of the states. (American Institute of Physics, 2000)
   Mass and density are the same thing.

Materials:

Baby oil	Rubbing alcohol
Food coloring	Clear, screw-top bottle (i.e., a small juice bottle)
Balance - See Activity Two	

Masses - small washers (outside diameter 7/8 inch (2.2 cm) or in-side hole diameter 3/8 inch (1 cm). Three of these small washers weigh approximately 1 gram. A nickel weighs approximately 5 grams. Calibrated measuring cup (240 ml = 1 cup)
Goggles are recommended.

Actual Washer Size

Science Skills:
   Students will be **observing**, **making predictions**, and **formulating a hypothesis and questions** about the behavior of two liquids **by manipulating materials to conduct an experiment** and **using numbers to measure** volume and mass and **calculate** density. Students will be **creating a model** and **collecting, recording**, and **interpreting data** and **developing the vocabulary to communicate** the results of their findings. Based on their findings, students will make an **inference** that mass and, therefore, matter is not gained or lost when the liquids are mixed.

Content Background:
   Liquids have a definite volume but no definite shape. Liquids will take up the same amount of space but will take the shape of the container in which they are placed. At the molecular level, the liquids have a low cohesive force, so the molecules of a liquid are spread far enough apart that they can flow over each other and move a little faster than in a solid.
   Physical properties of matter, such as mass, volume, and density can be measured and observed. **Mass** is the amount of matter present, and it remains constant. Mass can be measured with a balance. The metric basic unit of measure for mass is the **gram**. **Volume** is how much space something takes up, and the basic metric unit of measure for volume is the **liter**. **Density** is the amount of mass in a given space and can be determined by calculating the relationship

Name: _____ Date: _____

Student Inquiry Activity 4 : Making Waves (cont.)

between mass and volume. It can be calculated by dividing the mass by the volume.

$$\textbf{Density} = \frac{\textbf{Mass}}{\textbf{Volume}} \qquad \text{OR} \qquad D = \frac{M}{V}$$

For example, the mass of 1 milliliter of water is 1 gram at 4 degrees Celsius. The density of water is calculated by:

$$D = \frac{1 \text{gram}}{1 \text{ milliliter}} \qquad \text{OR} \qquad \text{a Density of 1g/ml}$$

Knowing the relationship of mass to volume or density, one can determine whether or not an object will sink or float.

This activity examines a mixture. A **mixture** is made when two or more substances are physically combined but not chemically joined together. The substances still have the same properties as before they were combined and can be separated by ordinary physical means. Other physical characteristics of matter include adhesion and cohesion. **Adhesion** is the attraction between unlike substances. Adhesion is why water and nutrients rise in plant stems. This concept explains why colored water seems to climb up a paper towel. **Cohesion** is the attraction of like substances. Cohesive forces allow you to add more water to a glass that is level full and make a dome of water on top. It is also the reason three streams of water merge into one stream when they are close together.

Challenge Question:

Why does one liquid consistently float and another one sinks to the bottom whenever they are mixed together?

Procedure: Goggles are recommended.

1. Measure 240 ml of rubbing alcohol (The volume of liquids may vary depending on the size of the bottle used. Use equal amounts of each liquid.)
   Reminder: When measuring liquid volume, you read the measurement from the bottom of the meniscus. The meniscus is the curve formed because of the adhesion of the liquid to the container. Adhesion is the attraction that two different kinds of molecules have for each other.

2. Add three drops of food coloring to the alcohol.
3. Measure 240 ml of baby oil. (The volume of liquids may vary depending on the size of the bottle used. Use equal amounts of each liquid.)
4. Find the mass of the liquids (by using the simple balances constructed in Activity Two).

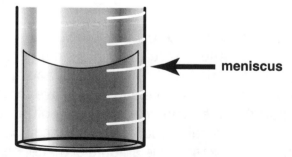

meniscus

Name: _____ Date: _____

Student Inquiry Activity ▮4▮: Making Waves (cont.)

NOTE: In finding the mass of a liquid, you must first find the mass of the empty container. Find the mass of the liquid and the container and subtract the mass of the container to get the mass of the liquid only.

5. Record the data in the data table below.
6. Predict what the volume and mass would be if you combined the two liquids.

Predicted volume of rubbing alcohol + baby oil _____ ml

Predicted mass of rubbing alcohol + baby oil _____ g (3 washers =1 g)

Calculate the mass and volume.

Liquid Density Exploration/Data Collection

Liquid	Volume (ml)	Mass (g)	Density (m/v)
Rubbing alcohol			
Baby oil			
Calculated alcohol volume + baby oil volume			
Calculated alcohol mass + baby oil mass			

7. Mix the two liquids together in the bottle.
8. Find the volume of the combined liquids.
9. Screw the cap on tightly so it seals.
10. Find the mass of the combined liquids.

Mixed Solution	Calculated Volume from above	Actual Volume (ml)	Calculated Mass from above	Actual Mass (g)
Rubbing alcohol + baby oil				

Name: _____ Date: _____

Student Inquiry Activity 4 : Making Waves (cont.)

Conclusions:

1. Compare the mass and volume of the rubbing alcohol/baby oil mixture. Were the combined masses and volumes the same as combining the original masses and volumes? Explain.

   _____

   _____

   _____

   _____

2. The law of the conservation of matter states that matter cannot be gained or lost. How is this related to your results?

   _____

   _____

   _____

   _____

3. Describe what happens when the two liquids are mixed. _____

   _____

   _____

   _____

   _____

4. Be sure the lid is on securely. Move the bottle around and describe what you see. Shake the bottle and let it sit for a few minutes. Describe what happens.

   _____

   _____

   _____

5. Why do you think this happens? _____

   _____

   _____

   _____

Name: _____ Date: _____

Student Inquiry Activity 4 : Making Waves (cont.)

Summary:

The food coloring mixes with the alcohol and not the baby oil. The baby oil is denser than the alcohol and consistently goes to the bottom, and the alcohol is less dense and therefore goes to the top. The combined mass and volume of the two liquids should be equal to the addition of the mass and volume found in the first part of the activity. This demonstrates the conservation of mass and volume when the two substances were mixed. Due to differences in density and the cohesive forces of the oil, oil and alcohol will not mix. Cohesion is the attraction molecules of the same substance have for each other.

When the bottle with the baby oil and alcohol is moved, waves can be formed. If the bottle is shaken, spheres may appear suspended in the oil or where the oil and alcohol meet. If allowed to sit, the two liquids should separate again.

Real-World Application:

Oil slicks on ocean water will float on the surface because they are less dense than the salt water. Due to the difference in density and cohesive forces of the oil, the oil and water do not mix.

Integration:

Other content areas connected to this activity might include proportional reasoning and oceanography.

Extensions:

The model developed can be used to study wave motion.

Name: _____ Date: _____

Student Inquiry Activity 4: Making Waves (cont.)

Liquid Density Assessment Rubric:

Use the following guidelines to assess student performance in this activity. Assign points depending on the mastery of these skills.

4 points	3 Points	2 Points	1 Point
• Volumes were measured accurately from the bottom of the meniscus. • Masses of the two liquids were measured within 0.3 g (1 washer) of the correct mass. • Densities were calculated correctly using **D = M/V**. • The masses stayed the same and it was inferred that matter was conserved when the substances were mixed. • The cohesive forces of the oil and alcohol are strong enough that they do not mix. • States that the oil is denser than the alcohol because it always sinks to the bottom of the bottle. Alcohol always goes to the top and is less dense.	• Volumes were measured accurately. • Masses of the two liquids were measured with more than 0.3 g difference • Densities were calculated correctly using **D = M/V**. • The masses stayed the same. There was no reference that matter was conserved when the substances were mixed. • Cohesion was mentioned. • Oil is denser than the alcohol because it always sinks to the bottom of the bottle. Alcohol always goes to the top and is less dense.	• Volumes were measured. • Masses were measured. • Densities were calculated. • Masses stayed the same. • No reference to cohesion. • Oil always sinks to the bottom of the bottle. Alcohol always goes to the top.	• Volumes were measured. • Masses were measured. • Densities were not calculated. • Masses stayed the same. • No reference to cohesion. • Did not know which was on the top or bottom.

Name: _____ Date: _____

Student Inquiry Activity 5 : What Sinks or Floats?

Topic: Chemistry—Solid Density, Buoyancy

Standards:
    NSES Unifying Concepts, (A), (B),(E)
    NCTM Number and Operations, Measurement, Data Analysis and Probability

Naive Concepts:
    Mass and volume are the same property.
    Relative particle spacing among solids, liquids, and gases (1:1:10) is incorrectly perceived and not generally related to the density of the states. (American Institute of Physics, 2000)
    Mass and density are the same things.

Materials:
    Tub 1/2–3/4 full of water (i.e., dish pan)
    Various objects (i.e., blocks, balls, rocks, etc.)
    15 ml water
    Balance - See Activity Two
    Masses - Small washers (outside diameter 7/8 inch (2.2 cm) or in-side hole diameter 3/8 inch (1 cm). Three of these small washers weigh approximately 1 gram. A nickel weighs approximately 5 grams.
    Calibrated measuring cup (240 ml = 1 cup)
    Measuring spoons (1 tsp = 5 ml)
    Film canister or some other small container.
    Goggles are recommended.

Actual Washer Size

Science Skills:
    Students will be **observing**, **making predictions**, and **formulating a hypothesis and questions** about density and sinking and floating **by manipulating materials to conduct an experiment**, **using numbers to measure** volume and mass. Students will be **collecting**, **recording**, and **interpreting data** and **developing vocabulary to communicate** the results of their findings. Based on their findings, students will be able to **predict** what will sink and float in water.

Content Background:
    Solids have a definite shape and volume. This means that solids keep their shape and take up the same amount of space. Solids have a high cohesive force, so the molecules of solids are packed tightly together. The cohesive force is the attraction of like substances. Molecules are in constant motion; however, in solids, the molecules are moving so slowly you cannot see them move.
    Liquids have a definite volume but no definite shape. Liquids will take up the same amount of space but will take the shape of the container in which they are placed. At the molecular level, the liquids have a low cohesive force, so the molecules of a liquid are spread far enough apart that they can flow over each other, and they are moving a little faster than in a solid.

41

Name: _____ Date: _____

Student Inquiry Activity 5 : What Sinks or Floats? (cont.)

Physical properties of matter, such as mass, volume, and density, can be measured and observed. **Mass** is the amount of matter present, and it remains constant. Mass can be measured with a balance. The metric basic unit of measure for mass is the **gram**. **Volume** is how much space something takes up, and the basic metric unit of measure for volume is the **liter**. **Density** is the amount of mass in a given space and can be determined by calculating the relationship between mass and volume. It can be calculated by dividing the mass by the volume.

$$\text{Density} = \frac{\text{Mass}}{\text{Volume}} \qquad \text{OR} \qquad D = \frac{M}{V}$$

For example, the mass of 1 milliliter of water is 1 gram at 4 degrees Celsius. The density of water is calculated by:

$$D = \frac{1 \text{ gram}}{1 \text{ milliliter}} \qquad \text{OR} \qquad \text{a Density of 1g/ml}$$

Knowing the relationship of mass to volume or density, it is possible to determine whether or not an object will sink or float.

Challenge Question:
    Why do objects sink or float?

Procedure:
1. Find the mass of each object.
2. Find the volume of each object.

Reminder: When measuring liquid volume, you read the measurement from the bottom of the me-niscus. The meniscus is the curve formed be-cause of the adhesion of the liquid to the con-tainer. Adhesion is the attraction that two differ-ent kinds of molecules have for each other.

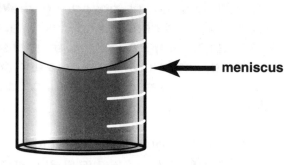

← meniscus

NOTE: Regularly-shaped objects, such as a cube, may be calculated mathematically. To determine the volume of a cube, multiply the length times the width times the height. For an irregu-larly-shaped object (i.e., a rock), volume may be found through a process called **displace-ment**. In displacement, a volume of water is measured. The object is placed in the water, and the volume is measured again. The difference between the second measurement and the first measurement is the volume of the object.

42

Name: _____ Date: _____

Student Inquiry Activity **5**: What Sinks or Floats? (cont.)

Exploration/Data Collection:
1. Record the mass and volume in the data table.
2. Find the density of each object/substance by dividing the mass by the volume.

Mass, Volume, Density

Object/Substance	Mass (g)	Volume (ml)	Density M/V (g/ml)
Water		15 ml	

3. Graph the results.

Mass and Volume Graph

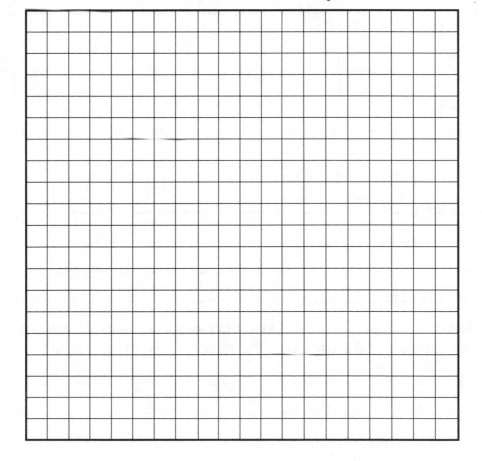

Mass

Volume (ml)

Name: _____ Date: _____

Student Inquiry Activity 5: What Sinks or Floats? (cont.)

4. Using the information illustrated by the *Mass and Volume* graph above, predict and record which objects will sink and which ones will float in water. Why?
5. Record the density of each object/substance in the data table below.
6. Test your predictions in the tub of water, and record the actual results.

Sink or Float?

Object/ Substance	Prediction Sink/Float	Actual Sink/Float	Why will it sink/float?	Density
Water				

Conclusions:

1. Were your predictions correct? Explain.

_____

_____

_____

_____

2. Examine the data table for "Sink or Float?" Is there a correlation between what sinks and what floats in water and the density of the object? How do you know?

_____

_____

_____

_____

Name: _____ Date: _____

Student Inquiry Activity 5: What Sinks or Floats? (cont.)

Summary:

Density is the amount of mass that is packed into a specific amount of space or the amount of molecules packed into a certain amount of space. The relationship of the mass and the volume will determine the density. Density is calculated by dividing the mass by the volume. Water has a density of 1 g/ml. Anything with a density greater than 1 g/ml will sink, and anything with a density less than 1 g/ml will float. On the graph, anything above the water line sinks, and everything below the line floats.

Real-World Application:

Density is used by scientists to help identify what substances are and by engineers when they select appropriate materials for construction.

Integration:

Social Studies - History of boat design

Technological design - Selecting the right materials for construction based on the properties of the materials

Extensions:

Use an orange as one of your objects. Once you have found the mass, volume, and density, predict whether or not the orange will sink or float. Test your prediction. What would happen if the orange was peeled—would it sink or float? Why? Try it. What happens? Why? Write your conclusions on your own paper.

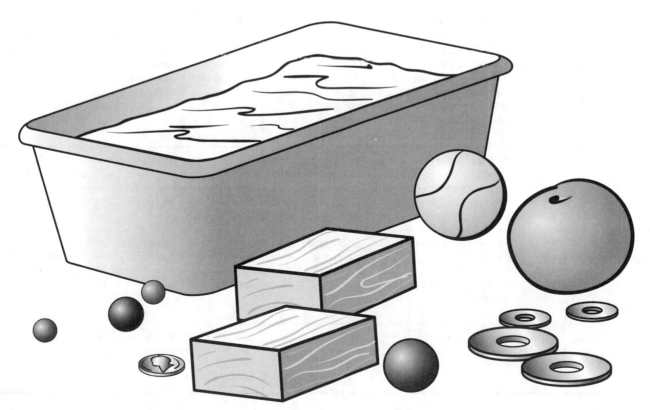

Name: _____ Date: _____

Student Inquiry Activity 5 : What Sinks or Floats? (cont.)

What Sinks or Floats? Process Assessment Rubric:

Use the following guidelines to assess student performance on this activity. Award points for the corresponding level of mastery for each skill.

Skill	4 points	3 Points	2 Points	1 Point
Observing	Observes test of all objects sinking and floating and records all observations	Observes test of all objects sinking and floating and records some observations	Observes test of all objects sinking and floating and does not record observations	Observes test of some objects sinking and floating
Classifying	Classified all objects in sink or float categories correctly	Classified all objects in sink or float categories	Classified some objects in sink or float categories	Grouped objects in categories
Predicting	Predicted correctly whether or not all objects would sink or float	Predicted correctly whether or not some of the objects would sink or float	Predicted whether or not all objects would sink or float	Predicted whether or not some objects would sink or float
Inferring	Based on the data table and graph, student could correctly predict whether or not all five of the objects would sink or float and explain reasons	Based on the data table and graph, student could correctly predict whether or not three of the objects would sink or float and explain reasons	Based on the data table and graph, student could correctly predict whether or not one of the objects would sink or float and explain reasons	Based on the data table and graph, student could correctly predict which objects would sink or float
Formulating Hypothesis	Forms an hypothesis about the relationship of density and sinking/floating and is able to explain the reasons behind it	Forms an hypothesis about sinking/floating and is able to explain the reasons behind it	Forms an hypothesis about sinking and floating	Makes an attempt to form an hypothesis about the relationship of sinking and floating
Experimenting	Follows directions; manipulates materials; performs trial-and-error investigations to find out what sinks and floats; formulates valid conclusions about the relationship of density and sinking and floating	Performs trial-and-error investigations to find out what sinks and floats; formulates valid conclusions about the relationship of density and sinking and floating	Follows directions; manipulates materials; performs trial-and-error investigations to find out what sinks and floats	Performs trial-and-error investigations to find out what sinks and floats
Measuring	Accurately measures the mass and volume of each object; uses measurement instruments properly; uses standard units	Accurately measures the mass and volume of some objects; uses measurement instruments properly; uses standard units	Measures the mass and volume of each object; uses measurement instruments properly; uses standard units	Measures the mass and volume of some objects; uses measurement instruments properly, uses standard units
Collecting, recording, and interpreting data	Collects useable data; correctly constructs and interprets graph of relationship of mass and volume; makes valid interpretations of data	Collects useable data; constructs and interprets graph of relationship of mass and volume; makes interpretations of data	Collects data; constructs and interprets graphs; makes interpretations of data	Collects data; constructs and interprets graphs
Communicating	Describes and transmits all necessary information accurately	Describes and transmits information to others	Describes information in responses on paper	Describes information

46

Name: _____ Date: _____

Student Inquiry Activity 6 : Moving to a New State

Topic: Chemistry—Change of State

Standards:
   NSES Unifying Concepts and Processes, (A), (B)
   NCTM Geometry

Naive Concepts:

Expansion of matter is due to expansion of particles rather than to increased particle spacing.
Particles of solids have no motion.
Relative particle spacing among solids, liquids, and gases (1:1:10) is incorrectly perceived and not generally related to the density of the states.
Materials can only exhibit properties of one state of matter.
Melting/freezing and boiling/condensation are often understood only in terms of water.
There is no difference between atoms and molecules. (American Institute of Physics, 2000)

Materials:

Ice	Resealable bag
Thermometer	Light source
Balance, constructed in "Is Air Matter?" activity	

Goggles are recommended.

Science Skills:

Students will be **observing** ice change from a solid to a liquid, **using numbers**, and **measuring** time and temperature as the ice changes. Students will be **inferring** what causes the states of matter to change from one form to another. They will be **manipulating materials** to make **predictions**, **develop questions**, **identify and control variables**, and **conduct an experiment** to determine what changes ice from a solid to a liquid. Students will be **communicating** and **developing vocabulary** during the process of **collecting**, **recording**, **analyzing**, and **interpreting data**.

Content Background:

Matter is defined as anything that has mass and takes up space or has volume. Matter has been classified into four states or phases of matter: solid, liquid, gas, and plasma. This book focuses on three of these states of matter because the concept of plasma is too abstract for students of this age.

Solids have a definite shape and volume. This means that solids keep their shape and take up the same amount of space. Solids have a high cohesive force, so the molecules of solids are packed tightly together. The cohesive force is the attraction of like substances. Molecules are in constant motion; however, in solids, the molecules are moving so slowly you cannot see them move.

Liquids have a definite volume but no definite shape. Liquids will take up the same amount of space but will take the shape of the container in which they are placed. At the molecular

Name: _____ Date: _____

Student Inquiry Activity 6 : Moving to a New State (cont.)

level, the liquids have a low cohesive force, so the molecules of a liquid are spread far enough apart that they can flow over each other, and they move a little faster than in a solid.

Gases have no definite volume or shape. The cohesive force of gases is almost nonexistent, so the molecules are not attracted to each other. The gases will expand to fill any container and will take the shape of the container.

Plasma has no definite shape or volume and is a highly energized gas. As with any gas, the cohesive force of plasma is almost nonexistent, so the molecules are not attracted to each other. The gases will expand to fill any container and will take the shape of the container.

Matter can undergo different kinds of changes—physical, chemical, and nuclear. A **physical change** is an alteration in a substance that does not change the chemical makeup of the substance. Ice changing into water is a physical change. Physical changes include changes in states of matter. Heat is added or taken away when matter changes from one state to another. Evaporation, condensation, and sublimation are processes of these changes in state. **Evaporation** is the process of a liquid changing to a gas when it is heated. When alcohol is placed on your body, it has a cooling sensation because the heat in your body causes the alcohol to quickly change into a gas. **Condensation** is the process of a gas changing to a liquid when it is cooled. When warm breath comes in contact with a cold window, the water vapor in it condenses on the window. **Sublimation** is when a solid changes directly to a gas without changing to a liquid first. Mothballs change to a gas through the process of sublimation.

Challenge Question:

How is matter changed from one state to another?

Procedure: Goggles are recommended.
1. Place an ice cube in a resealable freezer bag.
2. Measure the temperature of the ice.
3. Find the mass of the ice and bag.
4. Let the ice in the bag sit on the counter 5 minutes.
5. Check the bag after every minute.
6. Write a description of the ice and record the temperature in the data table below.

Moving to a New State Data Table

Time (Minutes)	Description	Temperature (°C)	Mass (Washers)
1			
2			
3			
4			
5			

Name: _____ Date: _____

Student Inquiry Activity **6** : Moving to a New State (cont.)

Exploration/Data Collection:

1. Describe ways that you might make the ice melt faster.

    _____

    _____

    _____

    _____

2. Select one of your ideas and write a hypothesis.

    Hypothesis: Ice will melt faster if I _____

    _____

3. Test your hypothesis.

4. Did the ice melt faster? Why? _____

    _____

    _____

    _____

5. Once the ice is melted, find the mass of the bag and water (liquid). Has the mass changed?

    _____

    _____

6. Measure the temperature of the liquid. _____ °Celsius.

7. Predict what you think would happen if you placed the bag near a light source and left it over time. What do you think will happen?

    _____

    _____

    _____

    _____

8. Test your prediction. Write down what happened. Was your prediction correct?

    _____

    _____

    _____

Name: _____ Date: _____

Student Inquiry Activity 6 : Moving to a New State (cont.)

9. Predict what will happen if you put the resealable bag back into the freezer? Why?

_____

_____

_____

Conclusions:

1. What can you infer about changing from one state of matter (ice, a solid) to another (water, a liquid)?

_____

_____

_____

2. Does the mass change when a substance changes from one form to another? How do you know?

_____

_____

3. How can you change water vapor back to a liquid?

_____

_____

4. How can you change water into a solid?

_____

_____

Summary:

    When the ice is heated, it will change to water. It will melt faster if more heat is applied. More heat could be added by holding or bringing it close to a light or heat source. The hypothesis should suggest that it would melt faster if more heat was applied. Molecules of all states of matter are in constant motion. As the heat is applied, the water molecules start moving faster and bumping into each other and begin to spread farther apart. As the molecules spread farther apart, there is less cohesive force. Cohesion is the attraction of molecules of the same substance for each other. In a solid, the cohesive forces are strong. When the substance changes to a liquid or gas, the cohesive forces become lower and lower. If enough heat is taken from the water by putting it into the freezer, it will change back to solid ice. The temperature should increase as the ice melts. The mass should stay the same because there is no gain or loss of mass when substances change states. This is referred to as the Law of Conservation of Mass.

Name: _____ Date: _____

Student Inquiry Activity 6 : Moving to a New State (cont.)

Real-World Application:

Ice in a soft drink melts because it takes the heat from the liquid to melt the ice, and it makes the drink cooler.

Integration:

Earth Science: Weather related to water cycle

Extensions:

Put the ice in a heat-resistant container with a balloon over the top of the bottle and set it next to a heat/light source. The balloon captures the gas so it does not escape into the room. The balloon inflates as the water changes to a gas. This will also show the conservation of mass as a substance changes from a liquid to a gas. If the balloon is cooled, the gas should condense back to water.

Moving to a New State Assessment Rubric:

Use the following guidelines to assess student performance on the activity. Award points for the corresponding level of mastery of each skill.

___ **3 points**
- Constructs and clearly states the hypothesis. The hypothesis should suggest it would melt faster if more heat was applied.
- Was able to conclude that matter can change from one form to another by adding or taking away heat.
- Was able to apply what was learned in the activity by correctly suggesting that the water vapor could be changed back to a liquid and solid by taking away heat.
- Accurately collected, recorded, analyzed, and interpreted the data collected.

___ **2 points**
- Constructs and clearly states the hypothesis.
- Was able to conclude that matter can change from one form to another by adding heat and cooling.
- Was able to apply what was learned in the activity by correctly suggesting that the water vapor could be changed back to a liquid and solid by cooling.
- Accurately collected, recorded, analyzed, and interpreted the data collected.

___ **1 point**
- Constructs and states the hypothesis.
- Was able to conclude that matter can change from one form to another by adding heat.
- Attempted to explain but was not able to apply what was learned in the activity by correctly suggesting that the water vapor could be changed back to a liquid and solid by taking away heat or cooling.
- Accurately collected, recorded, analyzed, and interpreted the data collected.

Name: _____   Date: _____

Student Inquiry Activity 7 : Time for Tea—High and Low Tea

Topic: Chemistry—Diffusion

Naive Concepts:
   Mass and volume are the same property.
   Particles of solids have no motion.
   Relative particle spacing among solids, liquids, and gases (1:1:10) is incorrectly perceived and not generally related to the density of the states.

Materials:
   2 tea bags
   Warm and cold water
   2 cups
   Measuring cup
   Thermometer
   Goggles are recommended.

Science Skills:
   In this activity students will be **observing** what happens when tea bags are placed in warm and cold water, **using numbers to measure** the amounts of water used, **inferring** from their observations that substances flow from areas of high concentration to areas of low concentration (diffusion), and heat speeds up this process. Students will be **communicating** with each other while they are **manipulating materials**, **recording and interpreting data**, and **experimenting.**

Content Background:
   Diffusion is a physical change. The tendency of molecules to move from an area of high concentration to low concentration is **diffusion**. Putting a tea bag in water is an example of diffusion. The tea bag has a high concentration of tea; the water has a low concentration. The tea molecules then have a tendency to move into the water until there is an equal concentration in each. The temperature of the water determines how fast the diffusion takes place. Heat is also being exchanged in this action. Some of the heat from the water is being transferred to the tea in the tea bag. Heat can be transferred through conduction, convection, or radiation. **Conduction** is when heat is transferred by collisions of the particles of the substance. **Convection** is when heat energy is transferred in gas or liquid by the currents in the heated fluid. In **radiation**, energy is transferred by electromagnetic waves.
   A **mixture** is made when two or more substances are physically combined but not chemically joined together. The substances still have the same properties as before they were

Name: _____   Date: _____

Student Inquiry Activity 7 : Time for Tea—High and Low Tea (cont.)

combined and can be separated by ordinary physical means. Mixing table salt in water is an example of a mixture. The table salt dissolves in the water and seems to disappear. However, the table salt molecules actually take up the spaces between the water molecules. When the water is evaporated, the salt will remain. The table salt and water do not lose their own properties.

Challenge Question:
       Why does tea mix with water?

Procedure: Goggles are recommended.
1.   Place 250 ml of warm water in one cup.
2.   Record the temperature. Temperature of the warm water: _____ degrees Celsius
3.   Place 250 ml of cold water in another cup.
4.   Record the temperature. Temperature of the cold water: _____ degrees Celsius
5.   Put a tea bag in each cup and record the time.
6.   Record the time the bags were put into the cups of water. _____

Exploration/Data Collection:

Time (min.)	Warm Water Temperature (°C)	Observations	Cold Water Temperature (°C)	Observations
1				
2				
3				
4				
5				
10				

Name: _____ Date: _____

Student Inquiry Activity **7**: Time for Tea—High and Low Tea (cont.)

1. What happened to the cup of warm water? Why?

    _____

    _____

    _____

    _____

2. What happened to the cup of cold water? Why?

    _____

    _____

    _____

    _____

Summary:

    The tendency of molecules to move from an area of high concentration to an area of low concentration is diffusion. Putting a tea bag in water is an example of diffusion. The tea bag has a high concentration of tea; the water has a low concentration. The tea molecules then have a tendency to move into the water until there is an equal concentration in each. The temperature of the water determines how fast the diffusion takes place.

    The heat in the warm water acts as a catalyst to speed up the reaction. The molecules of the warm water are moving faster, so the tea diffuses faster.

Real-World Application:

    This activity demonstrates how tea and coffee are made.

Integration:

    Food Sciences

Extensions:

    Try other substances such as powdered fruit drinks, chocolate syrup, or other drink mixes.

Name: _____ Date: _____

Student Inquiry Activity 8 : Was It a Chemical Change?— How Do I Know?

Topic: Chemistry—Chemical Reactions; Endothermic and Exothermic Reactions

Standards:
NSES Unifying Concepts, (A), (B)
NCTM Measurement, Data Analysis

Naive Concepts:
Gases are invisible and are not matter.
Gases do not have mass.
Mass and volume are the same property.
Air and oxygen are the same gas.
Chemical changes are perceived as additive, rather than interactive. After chemical change, the original substances are perceived as remaining, even though they are altered.
Formation of a new substance with new properties is seen as a simple happening rather than as the result of particle rearrangement. (American Institute of Physics, 2000)

Materials
Note to teacher or other adults: This can be done as a mystery substance activity if the containers are numbered, or students can do this on their own.
10 ml White Powder #1 (Cheer™ powdered laundry detergent)
10 ml White Powder #2 (baking soda)
20 ml Clear Liquid #1 (water)
30 ml Clear Liquid #2 (vinegar)
Measuring spoons (5 ml = 1 tsp)
Resealable freezer bags
2 film canisters or small vials
Magnifying glass
Goggles are recommended.

Science Skills:
During this activity, students are **measuring** volume, **observing** what happens when two white powders are mixed with liquids, **inferring** why the temperature changes when the substances are mixed, and **predicting** what will happen when the second powder is mixed with the liquid. During this activity, students will be **communicating and developing vocabulary** such as *endothermic, exothermic, chemical change, compound,* and other words related to chemical reactions.

Content Background:
Properties of matter can be divided into two types—physical properties and chemical properties. **Chemical properties** allow substances to chemically react to other substances to form new substances. These changes occur at the atomic or molecular level.

Name: _____ Date: _____

Student Inquiry Activity 8 : Was It a Chemical Change? How Do I Know? (cont.)

Matter can undergo different kinds of changes—physical, chemical, and nuclear. A **physical change** is an alteration in a substance that does not change the chemical makeup of the substance. Ice changing into water is a physical change. A **chemical change** takes place when substances are combined, and they change their chemical structure. During a chemical reaction, atoms are rearranged into new substances. An animal digesting food is a chemical change. In a **nuclear change**, the change takes place in the nucleus of the atom.

A chemical change happens at the atomic level. A compound is two or more substances that are chemically combined to form a new substance. The structures of each of the substances change at the atomic level. This means they can only be separated by another chemical reaction. An example of a chemical compound is water. Water is made of hydrogen and oxygen; both are invisible gases at room temperature before they are combined. After they are combined, they form water, a clear liquid at room temperature.

Chemical reactions can happen spontaneously, or they may need some form of energy. Heat, light, mechanical devices, and catalysts provide energy for some chemical reactions. Some chemical reactions happen immediately, while some happen over time. Catalysts, increasing the surface area, increasing concentration, and heating are used to speed up reactions. How well these chemical changes occur is determined by how strongly the electrons are held in the outer shells of the atom.

Fire or burning is a chemical reaction. It is the process of the fuel combining rapidly with oxygen. This process is call **rapid oxidation**. Decaying plant matter, such as grass clippings in a garbage bag, will become warm, showing a chemical reaction is taking place. In this process, the plant material is slowly combining with oxygen; a process called **slow oxidation**. Rust is also an example of slow oxidation.

A precipitate is one indicator of a chemical change. A **precipitate** is an insoluble substance created during the reaction that settles out as a solid in the bottom of the container. Changes in temperature or color are also indicators that something has changed chemically. During a chemical reaction, heat may be given off or absorbed. If the heat is absorbed, it is an **endothermic reaction**; if it is given off, it is an **exothermic reaction**. If the substances give off an odor or gas, it is also an indication of a chemical change.

Challenge Question:

How do you know if a chemical change is taking place?

Chemistry

Student Inquiry Activity 8: Was It a Chemical Change?—How Do I Know?

Name: _____ Date: _____

Student Inquiry Activity 8 : Was It a Chemical Change? How Do I Know? (cont.)

Procedure #1: Goggles are recommended.
1. Closely examine White Powder #1 and the Clear Liquid #1; extend your senses by using a magnifying glass. Write down your observations.

_____

_____

_____

_____

2. Predict what will happen if you mix White Powder #1 and Clear Liquid #1.

_____

_____

Exploration/Data Collection #1:
1. Place 10 ml of White Powder #1 in a resealable freezer bag.
2. Pour 20 ml of Clear Liquid #1 in the film canister.
3. Carefully set the canister inside the bag with the white powder without tipping it over.
4. Zip the bag closed, pushing out as much air as possible.
5. Empty the film canister in the bag so it spills out into the bag.
6. Mix the two substances.
7. Describe what happens. Why do you think it is happening?

_____

_____

_____

_____

Procedure #2: Goggles are recommended.
1. Closely examine White Powder #2 and the Clear Liquid #2; extend your senses by using a magnifying glass. Write down your observations.

_____

_____

_____

_____

Name: _____ Date: _____

Student Inquiry Activity 8: Was It a Chemical Change?— How Do I Know? (cont.)

2. Predict what will happen if you mix White Powder #2 and Clear Liquid #2.

_____

_____

Exploration/Data Collection #2:
1. Place 10 ml of White Powder #2 in a resealable freezer bag.
2. Pour 20 ml of Clear Liquid #2 in the film canister.
3. Carefully set the canister inside the bag with the white powder without tipping it over.
4. Zip the bag closed, pushing out as much air as possible.
5. Empty the film canister in the bag so it spills out into the bag.
6. Mix the two substances.
7. Describe what happens. Why do you think it is happening?

_____

_____

_____

_____

Conclusions:
1. During endothermic reactions, heat is absorbed so the substances feel cooler. During exothermic reactions, heat is given off so the substances feel warmer. Which type of reaction, endothermic or exothermic, was each reaction? Why?

A.   Reaction #1: White Powder #1 and Clear Liquid #1.

_____

_____

_____

_____

B.   Reaction #2: White Powder #2 and Clear Liquid #2.

_____

_____

_____

_____

Name: _____ Date: _____

Student Inquiry Activity 8 : Was It a Chemical Change?— How Do I Know? (cont.)

2. Some indicators of chemical changes taking place include a change in temperature or color and gases or odors given off.

    A. In Reaction #1, did a chemical change take place? How do you know?

    _____

    _____

    _____

    _____

    _____

    B. In Reaction #2, did a chemical change take place? How do you know?

    _____

    _____

    _____

    _____

    _____

Summary:
    The first reaction was a combination of Cheer™ powdered laundry detergent and water. When the water is mixed with the powdered laundry detergent, heat is given off, so it is an **exothermic reaction**. In the second reaction, vinegar and baking soda were combined. The heat was absorbed; therefore, this is an example of an **endothermic reaction**. The air was pressed out of the bag before the substances were mixed in the second reaction. This was done so as the bag also began to swell, students would realize it had to be due to something given off during the reaction. In this case, the bag swelled because of the carbon dioxide gas given off when the baking soda and vinegar were combined. Both reactions are chemical reactions as indicated by the change in temperature. The second reaction also gave off a gas, which is another indicator of a chemical change.

Real-World Application:
    Baking cakes, cookies, bread, etc., are examples of chemical changes. The gases given off during the chemical reactions taking place make them rise as they bake.

Extensions:
    Try other powdered laundry detergents to see if they react the same way.

Name: _____ Date: _____

Student Inquiry Activity 8: Was It a Chemical Change?—How Do I Know? (cont.)

Endothermic/Exothermic Assessment Rubric:

Use the following guidelines to assess student performance on this activity. Check those statements that apply.

_____ Students were able to make detailed observations of what was happening in each reaction and were able to determine that a chemical reaction had taken place and what type of reaction it was.

Some indicators that students were able to do this are below.

Reaction #1 Observations

_____ The substances felt warmer after they were mixed.

_____ Inferred that Reaction #1 was an exothermic reaction.

_____ Inferred that Reaction #1 was a chemical reaction because there was a temperature change, which is an indicator of a chemical change.

Reaction #2 Observations

_____ The substances felt cooler and a gas filled up the bag when the two substances were mixed.

_____ Inferred that Reaction #2 was an endothermic reaction.

_____ Inferred that Reaction #2 was a chemical reaction because there was a temperature change and a gas was given off, both indicators of a chemical change.

Name: _____ Date: _____

Student Inquiry Activity 9 : Rusty Wool

Topic: Chemistry—Chemical Reactions; Oxidation

Standards:
    NSES Unifying Concepts, (A), (B)
    NCTM Measurement, Data Analysis

Naive Concepts:
    Mass and volume are the same property.
    Air and oxygen are the same gas.
    Chemical changes are perceived as additive, rather than interactive. After chemical change, the original substances are perceived as remaining, even though they are altered.
    Formation of a new substance with new properties is seen as a simple happening, rather than as the result of particle rearrangement. (American Institute of Physics, 2000)

Materials:
    WARNING! DUE TO THE MATERIALS USED, THIS ACTIVITY IS AN UPPER-LEVEL AC-TIVITY AND SHOULD BE MONITORED BY AN ADULT AT ALL TIMES!
    Goggles are recommended. Do not mix more than the recommended amounts. Do the activity in a well ventilated area. Use plastic gloves when handling the materials. Be sure to add all ingredients in the proportions given. Before disposing of the liquid waste material, dilute it with a lot of water to stop the chemical reaction.
    One small ball of steel wool   Paper towel (or coffee filter)
    Magnet   20 ml bleach
    10 ml vinegar   2 small jars
    Measuring spoons (5 ml = 1 tsp)   Candle
    Matches   Metal spoon
    Water (125 ml or approx. $\frac{1}{2}$ cup—enough to cover the small ball of steel wool in the jar)
    Plastic gloves   Goggles

Science Skills:
    Students will be **manipulating materials** to conduct an experiment on what makes rust. During this activity, students are **measuring** volume, **observing** what happens when a magnet is brought close to steel wool, inferring why an orange precipitate forms when the substances are mixed, and **predicting** what will happen when the orange powder is heated. During this activity, students will be **communicating and developing vocabulary** such as *precipitate, chemical change, compound*, and other words related to chemical reactions.

Content Background:
    Properties of Matter can be divided into types—physical properties and chemical properties. **Chemical properties** allow substances to react chemically to other substances to form new substances. These changes occur at the atomic or molecular level.
    Matter can undergo different kinds of changes—physical, chemical, and nuclear. A **physical change** is an alteration in a substance that does not change the chemical makeup of

61

Name: _____ Date: _____

Student Inquiry Activity 9 : Rusty Wool (cont.)

the substance. Ice changing into water is a physical change. A **chemical change** takes place when substances are combined, and they change their chemical structure. During a chemical reaction, atoms are rearranged into new substances. An animal digesting food is a chemical change. In a **nuclear change**, the change takes place in the nucleus of the atom.

A chemical change happens at the atomic level. A compound is two or more substances that are chemically combined to form a new substance. The structures of each of the substances change at the atomic level. This means they can only be separated by another chemical reaction. An example of a chemical compound is water. Water is made of hydrogen and oxygen; both are invisible gases at room temperature before they are combined. After they are combined, they form water, a clear liquid at room temperature.

Chemical reactions can happen spontaneously, or they may need some form of energy. Heat, light, mechanical devices, and catalysts provide energy for some chemical reactions. Some chemical reactions happen immediately, while some happen over time. Catalysts, increasing the surface area, increasing concentration, and heating are used to speed up reactions. How well these chemical changes occur is determined by how strongly the electrons are held in the outer shells of the atom.

Fire or burning is a chemical reaction. It is the process of the fuel combining rapidly with oxygen. This process is called **rapid oxidation**. Decaying plant matter, such as grass clippings in a garbage bag, will become warm, showing a chemical reaction is taking place. In this process, the plant material is slowly combining with oxygen; a process called **slow oxidation**. Rust is also an example of slow oxidation.

A precipitate is one indicator of a chemical change. A **precipitate** is an insoluble substance created during the reaction that settles out as a solid in the bottom of the container. Changes in temperature or color are also indicators that something has changed chemically. During a chemical reaction, heat may be given off or absorbed. If the heat is absorbed, it is an **endothermic reaction**; if it is given off, it is an **exothermic reaction**. If the substances give off an odor or gas, it is also an indication of a chemical change.

Some of the processes used by chemists are filtration, distillation, fermentation, and sublimation. This activity will use the process of filtration. **Filtration** uses porous materials to separate solids from liquids, i.e., a coffee filter allows the coffee oils through but not the grounds. **Distillation** is a process by which a liquid is turned into a vapor and condensed back into a liquid on a cold surface. This process is used to separate liquids from dissolved solids or volatile liquids from less volatile ones. For example, salt can be removed from seawater by allowing the water to evaporate. **Fermentation** is the production of alcohol from sugar through the action of yeast or bacteria. **Sublimation** is when a solid turns to a gas without first changing to a liquid, i.e., moth balls.

Challenge Question:

Why does the steel wool turn orange?

Name: _____   Date: _____

Student Inquiry Activity 9 : Rusty Wool (cont.)

Procedure:
WARNING! DUE TO THE MATERIALS USED, THIS ACTIVITY IS AN UPPER-LEVEL ACTIVITY AND SHOULD BE MONITORED BY AN ADULT AT ALL TIMES! Goggles are recommended. Do not mix more than the recommended amounts. Do the activity in a well ventilated area. Use plastic gloves when handling the materials. Be sure to add all ingredients in the proportions given. Before disposing of the liquid waste material, dilute it with a lot of water to stop the chemical reaction.

1. Examine the steel wool. Describe what the steel wool looks like.

    _____

    _____

    _____

2. Bring a magnet up to the steel wool. Is the steel wool attracted to the magnet? How do you know?

    _____

    _____

    _____

3. Pull off a small amount of steel wool.
4. Make a small ball of steel wool.
5. Place the steel wool in a jar.
6. Put enough water in the jar to cover the steel wool ball (125 ml or approx. $\frac{1}{2}$ cup).
7. Examine the steel wool in the water.
8. Describe what you see.

    _____

    _____

    _____

9. Let the steel wool sit in the water for five minutes.
10. Describe what you see.

    _____

    _____

    _____

Name: _____ Date: _____

Student Inquiry Activity 9 : Rusty Wool (cont.)

Exploration/Data Collection:
WARNING! DUE TO THE MATERIALS USED, THIS ACTIVITY IS AN UPPER-LEVEL ACTIVITY AND SHOULD BE MONITORED BY AN ADULT AT ALL TIMES! Goggles and plastic gloves are recommended.

1. Add 20 ml of bleach and 10 ml of vinegar to the water.
2. Describe what you see.

_____

_____

_____

3. Let the jar sit for 5 minutes. Describe what you see.

_____

_____

_____

4. Remove the steel wool from the jar.
5. Allow the liquid to sit until the mixture settles and an orange powder forms at the bottom of the jar.
6. Drain off the liquid carefully so you do not spill the orange powder out of the jar. Dilute the bleach/vinegar/water mixture with plenty of water before disposing of it to stop the reaction.
7. Fill the jar with the powder with water and stir it.
8. Allow the orange substance to settle to the bottom again.
9. Once it has settled out again, drain off most of the water as you did above.
10. Place the coffee filter in the other jar.
11. Pour the remaining liquid and powder into the filter.
12. Spread out the filter with the orange powder and allow it to dry.
13. Closely examine the orange powder. Describe what you see.

_____

_____

_____

14. Test the orange substance to see if it is attracted to a magnet.

Name: _____ Date: _____

Student Inquiry Activity 9 : Rusty Wool (cont.)

15. Write down your observations.

_____

_____

_____

_____

16. Place the orange substance in an old spoon.
17. Hold the spoon over a candle flame.
18. Observe the powder as it is heated. Describe what happens.

_____

_____

_____

_____

_____

_____

_____

19. After the orange powder has changed color completely, put the substance in the spoon out on the coffee filter again.
20. Describe what it looks like.

_____

_____

_____

_____

21. Test to see if it is attracted to a magnet. Write down your observations.

_____

_____

_____

_____

Name: _____ Date: _____

Student Inquiry Activity **9**: Rusty Wool (cont.)

Conclusions:

1. What happened during this investigation?

   _____

   _____

   _____

   _____

   _____

2. Why do you think the steel wool turned orange and left a powder in the jar?

   _____

   _____

   _____

   _____

3. Why did the orange powder change colors when it was heated?

   _____

   _____

   _____

   _____

4. Summarize what happened in the data tables below.

Steel Wool Investigation

	Steel Wool Characteristics
Before	
In Water	
In Solution with Bleach and Vinegar	

Orange Powder (Rust) Investigation

	Orange Powder Characteristics
In Water	
After Drying	
After Heating	

Name: _____ Date: _____

Student Inquiry Activity 9 : Rusty Wool (cont.)

5. When a chemical change takes place, new substances are formed that have different properties than the original substances. Using the data collected above, is this a chemical reaction? How do you know?

   _____

   _____

   _____

   _____

   _____

Summary:

When steel wool is placed in water for an extended period of time, it will rust. Rust is formed when iron combines with oxygen. This is a slow process under normal conditions. In this activity, bleach and vinegar are mixed with water, and one of the products formed is hypochlorous acid (HClO). The acid acts as a catalyst to speed up the reaction. A catalyst is a substance added to a reaction to increase the rate of reaction but is not used up in the reaction. The hypochlorous acid reacts with the iron (Fe) in the steel wool to form hydrated ferric oxide. ($Fe_2O_3 \cdot H_2O$) or rust. When the orange powder, ferric oxide, is heated, it is changed to a magnetic oxide of iron (Fe_3O_4), and it can then be attracted to a magnet.

This is an example of a chemical reaction because new substances are formed with different chemical and physical properties. In the first reaction, the steel wool changes color and an orange precipitate is formed, which is not attracted to a magnet. This orange powder is rust. In the second reaction, the orange powder changes to a blue-black color and the substance is attracted to a magnet.

Real-World Application:

Iron tools left outside in the rain for an extended period of time will eventually rust.

Integration:

Language arts writing in the content areas.

Extensions:

Determine the impact of using the hypochlorous acid as a catalyst. Put steel wool in water and leave it for an extended period of time making daily observations to find out when the rust would begin forming. Compare the time taken to form rust naturally with the time taken to form rust using the catalyst.

Name: _____ Date: _____

Student Inquiry Activity 9 : Rusty Wool (cont.)

Rusty Wool Assessment:

Successful students will complete the data tables and conclusion with the answers as follows.

Steel Wool Investigation

	Steel Wool Characteristics
Before	Blue-gray color, stringy, shiny
In Water	Blue-gray color, stringy, shiny; water made it look bigger
In Solution with Bleach and Vinegar	Turns orange; liquid becomes cloudy; orange powder forms on the bottom of the jar

Orange Powder (Rust) Investigation

	Orange Powder Characteristics
In Water	Looks like orange or red grains, solid particles, more dense than water
After Drying	Powdery, orange; is not attracted to a magnet
After Heating	Turns blue-black; is attracted to a magnet

5. When a chemical change takes place, new substances are formed that have different properties than the original substances. Using the data collected above, is this a chemical reaction? How do you know?

This is a chemical reaction. The steel wool changes texture and color when the bleach and vinegar are added. The orange powder (rust) formed in this reaction is not attracted to a magnet. When the orange powder (rust) is heated, it undergoes a second chemical change, it turns blue-black, and is attracted to a magnet. Since the properties of the substances involved in this investigation change their physical and chemical properties, a chemical change has taken place.

Name: _____ Date: _____

Student Inquiry Activity 10 : Why Does Popcorn Pop?

Topic: Chemistry Assessment—Change of State; Popcorn

Standards:
NSES Unifying Concepts and Processes, (A), (B)
NCTM Geometry – Use visualization, spatial reasoning, and geometric modeling to solve problems
See **National Standards Section** for more information.

Naive Concepts:

Expansion of matter is due to expansion of particles rather than to increased particle spacing.
Particles of solids have no motion.
Relative particle spacing among solids, liquids, and gases (1:1:10) is incorrectly perceived and not generally related to the density of the states.
Materials can only exhibit properties of one state of matter.
Melting/freezing and boiling/condensation are often understood only in terms of water.
(American Institute of Physics, 2000)

Materials:

Domed popcorn popper, air popper,
    or a pan with a clear lid
30 ml oil
120 ml popcorn
Navy bean

Science Skills:

Students will be **observing** popcorn popping, **using numbers**, and **measuring volume**. Students will be **inferring** what causes the states of matter to change from one form to another. They will be **manipulating materials** to **make predictions**, **develop questions**, **identify and control variables**, and conduct an **experiment** to determine why popcorn pops. Students will be **communicating** and **developing vocabulary** during the process of **collecting**, **recording**, **analyzing**, and **interpreting data**.

Content Background:

Matter is defined as anything that has mass and takes up space or has volume. Matter has been classified into four states or phases of matter: solid, liquid, gas, and plasma. This book focuses on three of these states of matter because the concept of plasma is too abstract for students of this age.

Solids have a definite shape and volume. This means that solids keep their shape and take up the same amount of space. Solids have a high cohesive force, so the molecules of solids are packed tightly together. The cohesive force is the attraction of like substances. Molecules are in constant motion; however, in solids, the molecules are moving so slowly you cannot see them move.

Student Inquiry Activity 10 : Why Does Popcorn Pop? (cont.)

Liquids have a definite volume but no definite shape. Liquids will take up the same amount of space but will take the shape of the container in which they are placed. At the molecular level, the liquids have a low cohesive force, so the molecules of a liquid are spread far enough apart that they can flow over each other, and they move a little faster than in a solid.

Gases have no definite volume or shape. The cohesive force of gases is almost nonexistent, so the molecules are not attracted to each other. The gases will expand to fill any container and will take the shape of the container.

Plasma has no definite shape or volume and is a highly-energized gas. As with other gases, the cohesive force of plasma is almost nonexistent, so the molecules are not attracted to each other. The gases will expand to fill any container and will take the shape of the container.

Matter can undergo different kinds of changes—physical, chemical, and nuclear. A **physical change** is an alteration in a substance that does not change the chemical makeup of the substance. Physical changes include changes in states of matter. The states of matter are solid, liquid, gas, and plasma. Heat is added or taken away when matter changes from one state to another. Ice changing into water is a physical change. Evaporation, condensation, and sublimation are processes of these changes in state. **Evaporation** is the process of a liquid changing to a gas when it is heated. When alcohol is placed on your body, it has a cooling sensation because the heat in your body causes the alcohol to quickly change into a gas. **Condensation** is the process of a gas changing to a liquid when it is cooled. When warm breath comes into contact with a cold window, the water vapor in it condenses on the window. **Sublimation** is when a solid changes directly to a gas without changing to a liquid first. Mothballs change to a gas through the process of sublimation.

Challenge Question:
Why does popcorn pop?

Procedure:
1. Examine the navy bean.
2. Split the bean apart. Describe what you see.

_____

_____

_____

_____

3. Examine the popcorn kernels.
4. Describe what they look like.

_____

_____

_____

70

Student Inquiry Activity 10 : Why Does Popcorn Pop? (cont.)

5. Based on what you found inside the bean, predict what might be inside the popcorn kernel.

_____

_____

_____

Exploration/Data Collection:

1. Based on your experience with popping popcorn and the activities you have just completed in chemistry, make a list of possible explanations as to why popcorn pops.

_____

_____

_____

_____

_____

2. Select one of your ideas and write a hypothesis. Remember, a hypothesis is a proposed explanation of an observation.

   Hypothesis: Popcorn pops because _____

_____

_____

3. What are some of the questions you might have to answer to find out if your hypothesis is correct?

_____

_____

_____

_____

_____

4. What variables do you need to control?

_____

_____

_____

_____

Student Inquiry Activity **10**: Why Does Popcorn Pop? (cont.)

5. Design an investigation to test your hypothesis. Describe step by step how you conduct your investigation.

_____

_____

_____

_____

_____

_____

_____

_____

_____

6. Use the data table below to write down your observations as the popcorn and oil start to get hot and the popcorn starts popping.

Time (min.)	Popper (pan and lid)	Popcorn	Oil
2 min.			
4 min.			
6 min.			
8 min.			
10 min.			

Conclusions:

1. Based on your investigation and observations, why does popcorn pop?

_____

_____

2. Was your hypothesis correct? Why or why not?

_____

_____

Name: _____ Date: _____

Student Inquiry Activity 10 : Why Does Popcorn Pop? (cont.)

3. How might you redesign your investigation? Use your own paper if you need more room.

_____

_____

_____

Summary:

The molecules in a solid are in constant motion even though you cannot see them moving. In a solid, the molecules have a high cohesive force; they want to stay close together, and the solid keeps its shape and volume. As you found out in the "Moving to a New State" activity, when substances are heated, the molecules are moving faster and faster as more heat is applied. As the molecules are moving around faster, they start bumping into each other, and the cohesive forces are not as strong. The molecules move farther apart, and the substance becomes a liquid and can no longer hold its shape. If the molecules are heated more, they become more and more excited and spread even farther apart. The cohesive forces are so weak that the substance changes into a gas and has no definite shape or volume. Gases expand to fill whatever space is available.

When the popcorn is heated, the molecules of the substance inside start moving around faster and faster, getting more and more excited. The solid substance inside becomes a liquid. As the liquid inside the kernel gets hotter, the kernels start to vibrate from the energy of the molecules bumping into each other inside. Finally, when the molecules of the liquid and the water inside get so hot that they can no longer be contained inside the kernel, they start popping out of the shell. The kernel has enough energy from the expansion of the water vapor and air inside that it can pop right out of the pan if the lid is off. As the popcorn starts popping, moisture collects on the lid of the pan. The water inside the kernels is so hot that it changes to a gas and rises to the top when the kernel pops. The lid of the pan is cooler than the inside of the pan, so when the water vapor hits the lid, it condenses or changes back to liquid water. If you find the mass of the uncooked popcorn and compare it to the mass of the cooked popcorn, it may seem like mass is lost. However, the Law of Conservation of Mass states that mass is conserved when matter changes form. The rest of the mass is there in the form of water.

Real-World Application:

Volcanoes erupt when the gases and hot magma inside the earth build up enough pressure that they can no longer be contained inside the plugged volcano.

When you shake a can of soda, the pressure from the carbon dioxide gas builds up and the soda sprays out when you try to open it.

Integration:

Botany – Plants: How Popcorn Grows
History/Social Studies – History of Popcorn

Extensions:

1. How long does popcorn take to pop?
2. What kind of popcorn pops the largest kernels?
3. What kind of oil works best?
4. How hot does the popcorn have to get before it starts popping?

Name: _____ Date: _____

Student Inquiry Activity 10 : Why Does Popcorn Pop? (cont.)

Why Popcorn Pops Assessment:

Mark the number of indicators students demonstrate to determine their mastery of each skill.

Process Skill	Indicators	All Are Seen	Over Half Are Seen	Half Are Seen	None Are Seen
Designing the Experiment	• Develops alternative ways to investigate a question • Manipulates materials • Performs trial-and-error investigations • Identifies testable questions • Designs own investigations • Formulates valid conclusions				
Hypothesis	• Constructs a hypothesis when given a problem or question • Formulates own hypothesis from own problem				
Identifying and Controlling Variables	• Identifies factors that will and will not affect the outcome of an experiment • Identifies variables that can be manipulated and those that can be controlled				
Inferring	• Describes relationships among objects and events observed • Uses all appropriate information in making inferences • Does not use nonexisting information • Separates appropriate from nonessential information • Exhibits sound reasoning in verbalizing inferences • Applies the process of inference in appropriate situations • Interprets graphs, tables, and other experimental data				
Observing	• Identifies objects • Uses more than one sense • Uses all appropriate senses • Describes properties accurately • Provides qualitative observations • Provides quantitative observations • Describes changes in objects				
Interpreting Data	• Identifies data needed and how to measure it • Collects useable data • Constructs data tables • Constructs and interprets graphs • Makes valid interpretations of data				

Bibliography

Children's Literature Resources:

Bowden, M. (1997). *Chemical Achievers: The Human Face of the Chemical Sciences.* Philadelphia, PA: Chemical Heritage Foundation Publication. A collection of photographs and biographies of chemists.

Bowden, M. (1997). *Chemistry Is Electric.* Philadelphia, PA: Chemical Heritage Foundation Publication.

Chemical Heritage Foundation (Summer 2000). *Chemical Heritage,* 18(2). Philadelphia, PA: Chemical Heritage Foundation.

Chemical Heritage Foundation (Fall 2000). *Chemical Heritage,* 18(3). Philadelphia, PA: Chemical Heritage Foundation.

Chemical Heritage Foundation (Winter 2000/1). *Chemical Heritage,* 18(4). Philadelphia, PA: Chemical Heritage Foundation.

Chemical Heritage Foundation (Spring 2001). *Chemical Heritage,,* 19(1). Philadelphia, PA: Chemical Heritage Foundation.

Chemical Heritage Foundation (Summer 2001). *Chemical Heritage,* 19(2). Philadelphia, PA: Chemical Heritage Foundation.

Chemical Heritage Foundation (Fall 2001). *Chemical Heritage,* 19(3). Philadelphia, PA: Chemical Heritage Foundation. *Chemical Heritage* is the journal for the Chemical Heritage Foundation.

Cooper, C. (1992). *Eyewitness Books: Matter.* London, England: Dorling Kindersley.

Feldman, A. and Ford, P. (1989). *Scientists and Inventors: The People Who Made Technology From Earliest Times to Present.* London: Godrey Cave Associates Limited.

Frese, G. (2000). *Dow Chemical Portrayed.* Philadelphia, PA: Chemical Heritage Foundation. This is a catalog for an art exhibit portraying the history of the Dow Chemical Company.

Hewitt, P., Suchocki, J., and Hewitt, L. (1999). *Conceptual Physical Science*. Menlo Park, CA: Addison Wesley Longman.

Hellemans, A. and Bunch, B. (1988). *The Timetables of Science: A Chronology of the Most Important People and Events in the History of Science*. New York, NY: Simon and Schuster.

Joly, D. (1988). *Grains of Salt*. Ossining, NY: Young Discovery Library. This book is the third book in the Young Discovery Library series.

Bibliography

Children's Literature Resources (cont.):

Lindley, E. (1996). *Chemistry: Common Misconceptions and Fairy Tales*. Available online at: http://people.we.mediaone.net/elindley/commiscn.htm

Newman, A. (1993). *Eyewitness Books: Chemistry*. London, England: Dorling Kindersley.

Rayner-Canham, M. and Rayner-Canham, G. (1997). *A Devotion to Their Science: Pioneer Women of Radioactivity.* Philadelphia, PA: Chemical Heritage Foundation.

Rayner-Canham, M. and Rayner-Canham, G (1997). *Women in Chemistry: Their Changing Roles From Alchemical Times to the Twentieth Century.* Philadelphia, PA: Chemical Heritage Foundation.

Rogers, K., Howell, L., Smith, A., Clarke, P., and Hederson, C. (2000). *The Usborne Internet-linked Science Encyclopedia*. London, England: Usborne Publishing Ltd.

University of Toronto (1998). *References for Misconceptions in Chemistry*. Available online at: http://www.oise.utoronto.ca/~science/chemmisc.htm

Wieland, P., ed. (1998). *Introducing the Chemical Science: A CHF Reading List.* Philadelphia, PA: Chemical Heritage Foundation.

Wertheim, J., Oxlade, C., and Stockley, C. (2000). *The Usborne Illustrated Dictionary of Chemistry.* Tulsa, OK: EDC Publishing. This reference is an illustrated guide of simple definitions of terms and concepts of chemistry.

Wilbraham, A., Staley, D., Matta, M., and Waterman, E. (2002). *Chemistry.* Glenview, IL: Addison Wesley.

Williams, T. (1987). *A History of Invention: From Stone Axes to Silicon Chips*. New York, NY: Facts on File Publications.

Software:

Dorling Kindersley. (1995) *Encyclopedia of Science.* New York, NY: Dorling Kindersley Multimedia.

Houghton Mifflin. (1997) *Inventor Labs: Technology.* Pleasantville, NY. Houghton Mifflin Interactive.

Houghton Mifflin. (1997) *Inventor Labs: Transportation.* Pleasantville, NY. Houghton Mifflin Interactive.

Bibliography

Software (cont.):

Microtel (1999). *The Science Club: Just a Chemical Reaction*. Montreal, Canada: Microtel Inc.

Stranger, D. (pub). (1998). *Thinkin' Science Series: ZAP!*. Redmond, WA: Edmark Corporation.

Websites:

www.pbs.org/wgbh/nova/lostempires/obelisk/
www.mos.org/sln/Leonardo
www.howstuffworks.com/
www.usborne-quicklinks.com
www.brainpop.com/science/seeall.wem
www.miamisci.org/af/sln/phantom/
www.mathmol.com/textbook/middle_home.html
www.iop.org/Physics/Electron/Exhibition/
www.pbs.org/wgbh/aso/tryit/atom/
www.exploratorium.edu/science_explorer/
www.its.caltech.edu/~atomic/snowcrystals
www.miamisci.org/af/sln/phases
www.funbrain.com/periodic/index.html
http://www.chemicalelements.com/
www.chem4kids.com/index.html

Curriculum Resources:

American Institute of Physics (2000). *Children's Misconceptions About Science.* American Institute of Physics. Available online at: http://www.amasci.com/miscon/opphys.html.

American Institute of Physics (Circa 1988) *Operation Physics: Matter and Its Changes*. American Institute of Physics.

Barber, J. (1986).*Chemical Reactions.* Berkeley, CA: Lawrence Hall of Science.

Chemical Education for Public Understanding Program. (Circa 1988). *Chemicals, Health, Education and Me.* Berkeley, CA: Lawrence Hall of Science.

Chemical Education for Public Understanding Program. (Circa 1988).*Chemical Education for Public Understanding Program*. Berkeley, CA: Lawrence Hall of Science.

Bibliography

Curriculum Resources (cont.)

Gertz, S., Portman, D, and Sarquis, M. (1996). *Teaching Physical Science Through Children's Literature: 20 Complete Lessons for Elementary Grades*. Middletown, OH: Terrific Science Press.

Glover, D. (1993). *Solids and Liquids.* New York, NY: Kingfisher.

Greenberg, B. and Patterson, D. (1998). *Art in Chemistry: Chemistry in Art*. Englewood, CO: Teacher Ideas Press.

Liem, T. (1992). *Invitations to Science Inquiry: Over 400 Discrepant Events to Interest and Motivate Your Students in Learning Science*. Chion Hills, CA: Science Inquiry Enterprises.

Lorbeer, G. (2000). *Science Activities for Middle School Students*. Boston, MA: McGraw-Hill.

Marsland, D. (2000). *Science and Technology Concepts for Middle Schools: Properties of Matter*. Burlington, NC: Carolina Biological Supply Company.

Sarquis, M. (1997). *Exploring Matter With Toys: Using and Understanding the Senses.* Middletown, OH: Terrific Science Press.

Sarquis, J., Hogue, L., Sarquis, M., and Woodward,L. (1997). *Investigating Solids, Liquids, and Gases With Toys: States of Matter and Changes of State.* Middletown, OH: Terrific Science Press.

Sarquis, M. and Sarquis, J. (1991). *Fun With Chemistry: A Guidebook of K-12 Activities, Volume One*. Madison, WI: Institute for Chemical Education.

Sarquis, J., Sarquis, M., and Williams, J. (1995). *Teaching Chemistry With Toys: Activities for Grades K-9.* Middletown, OH: Terrific Science Press.

Sherwood, M., (ed.) (1985). *Chemistry Today*. Chicago, IL: World Book Encyclopedia.

Taylor, B. (1998). *Teaching Energy With Toys: Complete Lessons for Grades 4-8*. Middletown, OH: Terrific Science Press.